P9-DHP-168

OUR COMMON LIFE

For Drew
with love
Bill

Also by William P. Mahedy:

Out of the Night
Rule of Life (Fall, 2007)

With Janet Bernardi:
A Generation Alone

Our Common Life

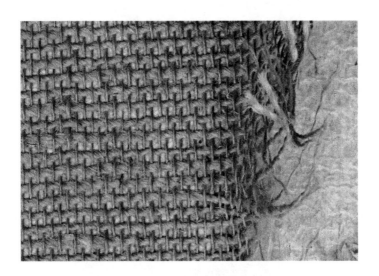

William P. Mahedy

Greyhound Books

Our Common Life

Published by:

Greyhound Books
2000 Stock Creek Road
Knoxville, TN 37920
865-405-3002
radixpress.com

All rights reserved. No part of this book may be reproduced or transmitted in any form or by any means, electronic or mechanical, including photocopying, recording, or by any information storage and retrieval system, without written permission from the authors, except for the inclusion of brief quotations in reviews.

Copyright 2006 by William P. Mahedy

ISBN: 1-59677-016-3
First printing, February 2007

Library of Congress Control Number: 2006941049

Dedication

This book is dedicated to the Augustinians. This includes those in the Order of St. Augustine and those who, like myself, are now "alumni" of the Order; the students in our schools, the faculty and staff with whom we have worked and those wonderful people with whom we formed a common life together.

our common life

Acknowledgements

This book would never have been written without the interest of Jack Deegan, O.S.A., my friend and former provincial of the Villanova province of the Augustinians. It sat on my computer as a collection of notes until my longtime friend and now my publisher and editor at Greyhound Books, Cynthia Mobley, insisted that I actually write the book.

The book could never have been written without the encouragement of my wife, Carol and the support of my family: Mike, Marie, Olivia, Steve, Devan and Nick. Our common life together is my primary source of strength.

My Augustinian roots go back to my childhood in St. Patrick's parish, my years at St. Augustine High School and Villanova University. These are all Augustinian institutions.

In those early years Vince McGarvey and John Aherne, both now in eternal life, stand out.

Augustinians Don Burt and John Driscoll assisted me greatly during my first year in the active ministry at Merrimack College. Mike Scanlon, seminary friend, has provided theological insights throughout the years. My contemporaries and lifelong friends in the Order, Walt Vogel and Tom Whelan have especially embodied the Augustinian common life for me.

My fifty year quest to understand and put into practice the Augustinian spiritual life began in the novitiate at New

7

Hamburg, New York with a series of conversations with John Keller, a fellow novice. We continued our discussions later on in the seminary, even collaborating on a paper to clarify the common life upon which we had embarked.

During my years of ministry in the Order and in the more than thirty years since I became an "alumnus," we have continued our friendship and our conversations, still trying to understand more deeply what the spiritual life is all about. Without John Keller's friendship and example, I would never even have thought about writing a book like this. The book is really a continuation of that long-ago and long-lost paper we wrote together. We've really been working on it together ever since.

Table of Contents

Introduction

American common life is disappearing. We Americans have always been "rugged individualists" but we have balanced this with a powerful sense of community.

But now that balance is disappearing. We are opting out of our compact with each other and are racing madly toward whatever we think will provide us individual satisfaction and fulfillment. Our social fabric is eroding. We are pulling down our safety nets, abandoning our public square and retreating behind our own walls.

American society has gone about as far as it can go on the path of individualism. Focusing on the "self" with our own individual wants and needs is healthy and good-but only up to a point. We have passed that point and are now on a long slide into a kind of collective narcissism.

Fortunately, countless people are now aware of what is happening to us and are searching for new directions. Many of us are trying to find ways to promote the common good. This book offers another way of viewing our common life and suggests some fresh directions we might take in our journey together.

First, a look at the problem: Why do I say that American community life is disappearing? Look around our cities. Fewer and fewer of us know our neighbors. Ethnic and racial enclaves are on the rise. The economic divide grows as wealth and income disparities increase. Political polarization and the culture wars are taking their toll. As the number of TV channels proliferates, we are able to watch only what suits us, so we no longer share the same network programs that everyone used to see and talked about. We are now able to sit in our living room "entertainment centers," and interact with the world from a distance. Or we can go online and get almost anything we want: news, entertainment, answers-it's all there and it's all solitary.

We are divided by music styles, clothes preferences, brand name choices and status. Religious divisions have arisen where none existed before. Inter-religious connections are frayed because of war in the Middle East and the role of Islamic extremists. The divide among American Christians is growing, no longer along denominational lines, but along a right-left demarcation. An arrogant, self-righteous, intolerant, harsh and punitive religious spirit is loose in the land.

Look at what is going on around us. In many parts of the country, traffic problems are getting worse. Drivers show fewer signs of courtesy or consideration. Refusing to signal a turn, cutting in and out of traffic, speeding, running stop signs and red lights: all are signs of diminishing care for one another.

For years I have done informal surveys. I talk to employees in all kinds of stores. I talk to barbers, nurses, teachers, construction workers, and supermarket checkout people and anyone else I come across in daily life. I listen to family members, neighbors and friends talk about their jobs and I hear a disturbing and constant theme.

It is clear to me that the bond that once existed between employer and employee has been destroyed. There is no loyalty, no commitment, and no mutual agreement between them. Once there was a common life in the workplace. It is no longer there.

Our lack of concern for one another at home and in the work place is reflected in our public life as well. Our infrastructure is declining. Overburdened roads, bridges and transit systems are rapidly deteriorating. Public universities, no longer adequately supported, are scrambling for private funds. Community colleges and K-12 public schools are so underfunded that, in most areas, teachers spend their own money on school supplies for their students. The idea that public funds should pay for the public good is now an alien notion.

Public agencies and private corporations alike have resorted to a "telephone tree" to deal with their constituents and consumers. Most of us have spent endless hours trying to figure out how the question we want to ask fits with the options given to us. Do we punch 2 or 3? Maybe it's really 6 that defines our problem. The voice on the phone assures us that all this is done "to better serve you," but we know this isn't true. It's because they really don't want to spend the money to hire enough people to talk to us. We are not really that important. Long customer service lines in stores reflect the same thing.

Somewhere around the fourth grade, we memorized the Preamble to the Constitution. We learned that a primary purpose of government was to "promote the general Welfare". But is this still true? I'm not sure that it is. The deterioration of common life pervades the government we've established as well as our society. Today, the purpose of government is to promote the welfare of those who can afford to purchase access to the administration and the Congress. Elected officials are no longer concerned about the general welfare. Oh, they pay lip service to it, but they really don't mean it. The premise that we have a common life together is no longer honored even by our own government. In all this there is a mean-spirited nastiness arising among us. We are becoming more confrontational, less tolerant and we really don't seem to care about each other.

For those among us who are Christian believers, it's becoming clear that we have to do something about this dangerous slide. When we see a problem clearly, we are able to look for solutions and move in new directions. We can, as the ancient poet says, "seize the day" and take another path. The opportunity to do so is here. We must return to the roots of our faith and discover again in these emerging and disturbing circumstances what it means to live in community with one another.

In order to do this in a practical way, deriving a useful "rule of life," something we can implement at home and at work, we must first examine the great themes of our faith. We must allow ourselves to be fascinated by the majesty and transcen-

14

dence of our beginnings. Look first at this:

"In the beginning was the Word, and the Word was with God, and the Word was God. He was with God in the beginning. Through him all things were made; without him nothing was made that has been made." (John 1: 1-3)

Now look at the immediate and practical punch line a few verses later in this passage.

"The Word became flesh and made his dwelling among us. We have seen his glory, the glory of the One and Only, who came from the Father, full of grace and truth." (John 1:14)

Here is the basis for our common life together. The eternal and Triune God, Father, Son and Holy Spirit, has made a common life with us through Jesus. All human community flows from this fundamental biblical truth.

In our exploration of our theme, we will use as a guide one of the greatest figures in Christian history: Augustine, a giant of the early Church. He was a thinker, writer and bishop whose impact upon the subsequent centuries is unequalled. For Augustine, our common life with God and our bonds with each other in community were two facets of the same inseparable reality. The spirit of Augustine provides an antidote to the pernicious effects of the unbridled individualism I have described above.

After his conversion to Christianity, Augustine wanted to live a quiet life in a community of friends, but this was not to be. His talents were so great that he was almost forcibly compelled to become a priest and then a bishop. He was involved in the great issues and controversies of his time. He was a theologian without peer in the western Church. His was an active life and it was long and fruitful (354 to 430 AD). His influence is still enormous and he is even being rediscovered today as a mentor and guide in a confusing and complex time. He is still, after more than fifteen centuries, a great teacher of how and why it is we live together with each other. He explained as well as anyone could, how it is that all of us are called to share, as "adopted children" through Jesus Christ, in the inner community life of God.

It was my privilege to have spent eighteen years in the Order of St. Augustine, a Roman Catholic religious community which followed the "Rule" Augustine wrote for his own community in the fourth century. In the thirteenth century, the Church gathered together several groups living a community life and asked them to work actively among an increasingly-mobile urban population. This new religious community was asked to follow the Rule of St. Augustine. From that time until now this community has been called simply The Order of St. Augustine, or simply "the Augustinians."

The first Augustinians were individuals so grounded in prayer they were sometimes known as "hermits." They banded together for community prayer so they were sometimes called monks. They were a combination of both, but their real missions were to be communities which went out into the streets of the then-emerging city-states to be in the midst of the people. They were to be an active presence in the world. They were to be the "leaven" in that turbulent and confusing era. They were to be "mendicants" in the sense that they would not

16

rely on their own property and personal goods. They were to be "beggars" because they relied for their support on the people they served. They were to be whatever they needed to be to proclaim the Gospel and serve the world. They could be preachers, teachers, cooks, gardeners, clergy or lay people. Their structure of self-governing was thoroughly democratic. They were to be creative and flexible. They were to be "on the move" and go wherever they were needed. Their life together was based on the principles of common life Augustine had set forth in the Rule and in his other writings. Following the example of Augustine, they were to embody active work with people, a deep prayer life and a common life together in community.

The Augustinian Order includes both men and women. The men came to be known by the distinctive name: "friars," which is derived from the Latin word for brothers.

At the time of this writing I have lived for more than thirty years after leaving the Order of St. Augustine. I am happily married. My wife and I have raised two children and we are now enjoying grandchildren. I have been accepted into the clergy of the Episcopal Church, and I have worked for many years in a non-church environment.

In all this, I find that I am still an Augustinian. I am still trying to balance the life of hermit, monk and friar in my approach to life. I believe that just as the world needed the friars in the thirteenth century, the twenty-first century needs the "brothers and sisters" out in the world to embody what it means to live a common life together.

Today, marriage and family are my primary communities. Our parish church has been a crucial community for our family. But the power of Augustinian common life goes beyond these intimate and obvious settings. I am continually amazed at how effective Augustinian principles are when translated into forming communities in places I have worked, in neighborhoods, schools and in political situations in which I have found myself.

The purpose of this book is to refer back to the Augustinian prism through which I have lived the Christian life and to share some ideas and practical suggestions that are applicable in our present situation. Augustinian spirituality is rooted in interpersonal relationships. That's what is missing today, as genuine interpersonal relationships degenerate into utilitarian transactions.

Where there is a decline in the quality of our life together, it is crucial that we formulate intentional strategies to restore and renew that common life.

The foundational principal in Augustine's Rule for community life: "Before all else live together in harmony (Ps 68:7) being of one mind and one heart (Acts 4:32) on the way to God." (Rule 1:2). In the rest of this book, I'd like to show you how that's possible in today's world.

One

Our Life Together: A New Vision and a Fresh Start

Where there is no vision, the people perish. (Prov 29:18)

Without a comprehensive vision, we do no more than stumble along in life from one incident to the next. So it was in biblical times and so it is today. Ezekiel, for example, saw the valley of the dry bones, but he also saw God bring the bones back to life and realized that the people of Israel would be restored.(Ez 37) Through that vision, the people saw that restoration would take place and they were able to act. With vision we grasp things in a new way. Real vision grips our intellect, emotion and imagination. Vision enables us to act in fresh ways. The Hebrew prophets envisioned a time when "the lion would lie down with the lamb" and when the "crooked ways would be made straight." These great visions lay at the heart of Israel's journey into God's future for them.

There are great political visions as well. The people of ancient Athens conceived of a democratic way that people might govern themselves. But these great visions, like that of Athens can wax and wane. Ancient Rome, which borrowed heavily from Athens, began as a republic, but ended as an empire in decline. Grand and sweeping visions can become distorted. Sometimes demagogues come along and seduce entire nations with grandiose visions that become socially and spiritually destructive.

Two examples of terribly destructive visions come to mind. In the early Twentieth Century, the Russian people were entranced by a vision of comradeship and equality between workers and owners which seemed to offer them hope in their impoverishment. The result was the Soviet Union and communism. After 72 years, millions of deaths, untold destruction and hardship, that vision was shown to be utterly false.

Similarly, Germans, defeated in World War I, ravaged by economic problems, tied their fates to a spellbinding orator who offered them a bright future. They anointed him as leader and followed him blindly. The monstrous evils spawned by the attempt to implement that vision ended in utter military and economic defeat for Germany and laid waste much of Europe.

Communism and fascism, the twin evils of the Twentieth Century, were each based on a vision that was conveyed brilliantly, imposed relentlessly and implemented ruthlessly. Spiritual death and moral bankruptcy, along with the horrendous effects of war, genocide and oppression were the price paid for attempting to follow visions at whose heart resided violence and willingness to exploit others.

What about us: we Americans? What is the vision which supports, nurtures and drives us?

william p. mahedy

The American Vision

America is the great melting pot, a very large pot containing a bounteous, delicious but complicated stew. We are not a homogeneous people. We come from different places; we inhabit different social, economic and emotional spaces. We are culturally diverse and religiously different. Though our first founders were English, down through the years our society has assimilated elements of many cultures, holding them together-always in some tension-but holding them together nonetheless.

Do we have a common vision at all? Is there a worldview that gives force and meaning to our lives, holding together the disparate elements of our life together as Americans? Is it possible? I believe there is such a vision, and it has been around for a long time.

Our American ancestors landed on a largely unexplored continent in the early Seventeenth Century. Most of them were from England. They spoke a common language and held similar values. Their great vision was that they were to be a "city on the hill" and a "beacon" to the rest of the world. This filled them with hope and optimism and inspired them to endure great hardships and to expand their settlements. But the vision was flawed. These early settlers committed the two American "original sins." They began the practice of slavery and they dispossessed the native peoples. But even with these terrible and tragic flaws, there was a real attempt to live a common life. Though slaves and the indigenous peoples were excluded from this common life, there was from the beginning an awareness that this was wrong. The slavery question was solved only by

21

a Civil War. Even after the Civil War it took another century to finally confront the plight of black Americans and their civil rights. The problem of the native peoples has really never been fully resolved.

Soon after the English colonies were established, people from other European countries began to come in large numbers to our shores. It wasn't long before the integration and assimilation of people from vastly different cultures became a part of the American experience-the so-called "melting pot." Here too there were problems, the exclusion of Chinese from California, for example. But over time we have made great progress. Through it all, our society has been remarkably resilient and we moved on to resolve truly momentous issues. When we decide to extend our vision to include more people within it, we move forward. When we narrow it, excluding others from the fullness of our common life, we create problems for ourselves.

The American paradox from the beginning has been that we are simultaneously very individualistic as a people and yet at the same time we value our common life together. Both these great ideas derive from the biblical vision and from Greek and Roman culture. Scripture is clear that we are created in the image of God as individuals. Each of us comes forth from the hand of God as a unique person. We relate to God and to each other always as individuals. But, it is also true that there is never a moment in biblical history, when individuals are not part of a community. Both Israel and the Christian Church are described as communities called into being by God. Biblical individualism is rooted in and is inseparable from community-a community with God and with each other.

22

william p. mahedy

Our American ancestors confronted the wilderness and all its problems, both as strong and hardy individuals, but also with a sense of solidarity and community. They banded together to build each other's homes and barns, they formed small communities on the edge of the wilderness. They held in tension these two elements of the life they had inherited. I remember stories told by my grandparents about their life on the western frontier in the 1870s and 1880s. Listening to them, I became aware that I was descended from people who had no fear of acting alone, and yet they were fully committed to the common good of the towns and the farm community in which they lived. These stories differ very little from what I have read and what I have heard from others. My wife's ancestors came west in covered wagons. The stories from her family are all about people, strong and hardy for sure, but always moving on together.

The abolition of slavery, first in England and then in the United States, derived its moral force and its spiritual energy from the biblical vision that we are all created in the image of God. Though some used Scripture passages to justify slavery, it became clear that the primary biblical emphasis on the common humanity of all people as God's creation had to prevail. Slavery benefited some individuals, but it was devastating to those held captive and it was ultimately destructive of the American common good. It had to end and many people at the time understood this.

When Abraham Lincoln tried to hold the nation together, he appealed in his first inaugural address to the "mystic chords of memory" which bound us together as a people. He could not have used this imagery were there not a real foundation for it. This appeal was unsuccessful and the war came. But even at the height of the war, Lincoln never forgot that we are a common people and our government exists, as he said at Gettysburg "of the people, by the people and for the people." At the end of the war, Lincoln could have imposed harsh measure on the defeated South, but he did not. He returned again to the theme of our common life together. A little more than a month before he was killed, Lincoln urged his fellow countrymen to "bind up the nation's wounds." Lincoln remains a powerful presence in our national life and it is worth remembering that he was not afraid to appeal to "the better angels of our nature."

"Better angels" still hover in our national soul. Those better angels that incline us toward our life together are predominant in our history. Our individualism has been rooted in community. Paradoxically, we are stronger as individuals when we are in community. This context of the individual in community more closely resembles the biblical vision than does the countervailing kind of individualistic isolation which is now struggling for the ascendancy. This is a technological age in which we have the means to isolate ourselves with a minimum of interaction, relating to others mostly on the Internet or by email. It is an age in which we can sample the world through our television screen, switching the channel when what we see displeases us. Though I love the Internet, wouldn't be without email and watch TV, it is clear that these are helpful adjuncts, enhancing communication, but they are not substitutes for real life personal involvement with people "in the flesh". When they become the prism through which we interpret life, then, we have a problem.

It is *this* part of our national self-understanding, individualism set within community, that is beginning to come unraveled. It is the "better angels of our nature" which are leaving us. We are now seeing destructive elements which have been there from the beginning, but which we have never truly faced now coming into dominance. This is the taproot of our current problems. We are losing our sense of individuals necessarily embedded in community. The richness of our life together is clearly diminishing.

Our Vision Fading

Many Americans now believe that something is greatly wrong in our land. Clearly and demonstrably, we are becoming more fragmented as a people. We are becoming more isolated as individuals. Neighbors in cities and suburbs rarely know each other. Family disintegration seems to be accelerating. The traditional compact between employers and employees has given way to a bottom line approach that treats workers as just another expendable, disposable resource to be used up and discarded for the sake of higher profits. Social institutions, once geared to assisting individuals, now seem to function more for the sake of the organization than for the citizen, client or customer.

Our common life together is dissipating. We are now more like free-floating individuals bumping up against one another in solitary and disjointed movements than communities of people with a real concern for one another.

On a global scale, the disintegration of international common life is evident. When the United States was attacked by terrorists on September 11, 2001, the community of nations rallied to our side. For a brief time, the world was one.

But that initial good will and solidarity has long since given way to cynicism both at home and abroad. The United States is now fighting a war based on lies and deception. Our leaders apparently see nothing wrong with torture as an instrument of interrogation. Our government even ships suspects off to countries with little regard for human rights for more vigorous questioning.

We used to tell ourselves that Americans do not do those kinds of things. We are more moral. The United States does not fight preventive wars. It does not use military force except as a last resort. We believed that United States does not commit or condone torture. We do not conduct widespread surveillance on our own people. We do not abandon the poor in our society. We do not allow large numbers of people to wander homeless among us. Work should be adequately compensated. People should be able to get health care. In times of natural disasters, we truly come together to rebuild stricken communities. We believed these things. We thought we were a moral beacon to other nations. But now as we confront the evidence of what we have become, we must reexamine both what we believe and how we live out our beliefs. We are beginning what will hopefully be a very salutary self-examination.

Institutions of global cooperation like the U.N., established under American leadership sixty years ago to enable a community of nations to function, are now disdained and disregarded. We no longer seem to honor the idea that we are part of a common life among nations.

How can we reconcile the "better angels" of our national vision with what we are now becoming? We can't. The chasm between who we believe we are and our conduct is destroying us.

Clearly we must evaluate our current practice in terms of our initial vision. In doing so, we must also admit the possibility that the self-image suggested by that vision has never been completely true.

Economic Injustice

Government no longer works for ordinary people. Tax cuts go largely to the rich. Spending cuts impact ordinary working people and especially the poor. Corporate influence controls the government and increasingly dictates policy. Not surprisingly, corruption abounds at all levels, becoming ever more blatant and "in your face." The health care system is coming apart with ever greater numbers of uninsured and with the scope of coverage rapidly diminishing with those fortunate enough to have health insurance. If we truly cared for one another, none of this could happen.

The number of people living in poverty grows each year, impacting especially women and children. Wages have stagnated to the point where they don't keep up with inflation. Couples holding two or even three jobs between them are now unable to afford food and housing. Pensions for retired workers have been eviscerated by companies, which claim they can no longer afford them. The traditional understanding between

27

working people and their employers seems to be in effect no longer. The natural environment that we all share together is increasingly despoiled to benefit those who can earn a profit from the despoliation. In almost every case we examine, the corporate interests prevail over ordinary people. This represents another failure of our common life together.

A part of our self-understanding has always been that we are a compassionate people. We have always honored and rewarded honest work. We believe we are a generous people, unwilling to allow others to suffer needlessly, always coming to the aid of those less fortunate than ourselves and providing help when needed.

To some extent, this American self-image is correct, but it has never been completely true. There is, and has always been, another, less generous and competing vision at work among us. We have now reached a point where our individual impulses, which might indeed be open and generous, come into conflict with that other reality fuelled by a competing, and much darker vision which also drives us.

During disasters, an individual's true qualities are exposed. The same is true with communities. Not long ago, we saw these two alternate visions of ourselves in stark contrast.

The Test of Katrina

Remember the responses of people to Hurricane Katrina? This was an event that dominated our television screens in August and September 2005. Katrina was a terrible natural disaster, but the preparation for and the responses to Hurricane

Katrina are inseparable from the way we normally do business.

What we witnessed on our television screens was ordinary people both suffering as victims and as helpers of those in need. We also watched how these same people interacted with the larger institutions we have put in place to serve us. Individuals thrust together under tremendously adverse conditions could actually form communities and help each other to safety, working against great odds to do it. The resilience and often the heroism of these people were compelling. They were behaving almost automatically according to beliefs they had previously assimilated. They were acting out of a powerful vision of how people should behave toward each other. Clearly they believed that we all share a common life together.

We also saw the other side of the coin when it became clear that even heroic efforts could not overcome the inertia and incompetence of large public and corporate institutions rooted not in a concern for the common good, but working only for their own self-preservation and gain.

Our life together may thrive among small groups of individuals, but it is largely thwarted when it confronts the structures we thought were there to enhance and enable the American community to flourish. These institutions, established to benefit the public now seem to operate according to a very different set of assumptions about the common good.

Society consists of many threads woven into a single fabric. People like the medical personnel whose commitment to their patients in the face of hunger and dehydration led them to give each other intravenous solutions so they could keep on working. People like that live all around us. We all know men and women like those who served in the tireless Coast Guard rescue teams. There are people like that all around us in our families, our neighborhoods and at work. Fortunately, the vision of common good motivates much of what we do.

Flawed humanity, sinfulness, greed and violence, constants of the human condition were also in evidence in the Gulf Coast during the storm and its aftermath. Some people in New Orleans took from stores the necessities they needed to save their lives. A few others descended into criminal looting. How does this differ from society at large? The executives of Enron and other companies, as well as some elected officials, are looters as well.

Hurricane Katrina allowed us to look at ourselves under very difficult circumstances. Fortunately, we are not forced into situations like that very often, but that extraordinary setting showed us something about who we are and the way we behave.

We can also see that part of the flawed government response to Katrina was a prior unwillingness to fund projects that would have likely prevented the full force of the disaster. Decisions had been made consistently over decades that resulted in a weakened infrastructure. Similar situations are found around the country. The New Orleans situation is not unlike my hometown's unwillingness to pay for adequate fire protection. San Diego has a very dry climate with winds that blow off the desert. Horrendous fires two years ago made us realize how inadequate our fire protections are. Unfortunately, San Diego's citizens want public services, but we refuse to pay for the personnel and infrastructure to provide them. So we await each fire season hoping for the best, but paying not a dime more in taxes. We want a common life together, but we don't seem to want it enough to fund it. In my home town, we talk a good game, but when it comes right down to it, what is good for me as an individual-a few dollars less in taxes-trumps what is good for us together-better fire protection. We may have a vision of a common life together, but not a very powerful one.

Hurricane Katrina showed that the incredible bureaucratic tangles that impeded the delivery of aid are not unlike or separate from the bureaucratic snafus encountered in ordinary life, for example trying to get insurance companies to pay claims or to surmount the obstacle of getting past the choices in a telephone tree. Large institutions in the private sector are as bureaucratic and difficult to deal with as are public agencies. It is more difficult all the time to get through to them and if you do, you may find helpful individuals trying to assist you, but as often as not they will be frustrated by their own system and its policies. They may want to help you but they can't. There are two competing visions of who we are and how we function and they are in serious conflict most of the time in a great number of transactions every day.

Most difficult to face perhaps is the fact that the plight of the poor, largely black population of New Orleans and the plight of the Mississippi poor is really a reflection of the way our economic system actually works. Though we are unwilling to admit it, economic self-interest drives the social engine. The result has been increasingly great financial gain for a few, economic stagnation for many and impoverishment for multitudes with an ever diminishing safety net for those who need it. Again we see many threads of a single fabric. The awarding of contracts for the cleaning up and rebuilding after Katrina, who was hired and who was not, the problem of health care for those deprived of it-all followed a familiar pattern that continues to emerge in our country. Were we driven by our better angels to bind up that part of the nation's wounds? Not really. Once again, we were shown two alternate visions of ourselves, but we did not choose the high road.

The source of the problem was well stated by Bill McKibben in an article published in *Harper's Magazine* in Aug. 2005 entitled: "The Christian Paradox: How a faithful nation gets Jesus wrong." Here lies the conflict between the two competing visions that thread their way down the centuries of American history. Though never a Christian nation, the United States has always had a large majority of Christians in it. McKibben's thesis is simple: If roughly 85% of Americans claim some form of Christian faith, how can we in our economic life depart so far from the biblical commands to love our neighbor as ourselves, to love those that hate us, to give justice to widows, orphans and the oppressed, to feed the hungry and clothe the naked? How can we forget the beatitudes so completely in our public life? How can we go so far in the opposite direction?

Another Way To Look At Where We Are

One stream of our national self-image does indeed come from the Old and New Testament Scriptures, but as early as our colonial era, that vision began to be mixed with another and quite contrary belief system. During the Seventeenth Century,

Americans, like their European cousins, became entranced by a new worldview emerging from the power of scientific discovery.

The scientific method of inquiry is necessarily limited to material things. It uses mathematical calculations and quantifies its findings. It depends on predictability and it requires efficiency.

Our difficulties began when the scientific method, which is the only method appropriate in the sciences, became the norm and standard for all other kinds of thinking. The problem is easily seen when one tries to describe the full range of something like love, using only a scientific kind of analysis. Pretty dreary!

A new philosophy, which appeared at about the same time through Rene Descartes, focused on the individual as norm and standard of existence. "I think therefore I am," was his famous dictum. The problem here is that the thinking "I" becomes the norm and standard of everything, rather than the "I" having to conform its thought to external reality.

These two streams gradually converged over the centuries. The "I" with all its thoughts, desires and feelings became enthroned at the center reality. At the same time, the range of thinking, imagining and envisioning was constricted. This gave birth to what has by now become radical individualism. The individual, now isolated, from others becomes the "Imperial Self" and is in competition with other selves. What is good *for me* began to take precedence over what is good for *us together*. It was always the case that individual selfishness and greed influenced much of human behavior. This is a constant of

33

human nature, but there were, prior to the Seventeenth century, some powerful belief systems preventing these darker forces within us from overflowing their bounds. From that time on, however, individualism has pre-empted the common good. Until very recently individualism has been kept in check to some extent by the simple fact that people lived together in small enough groups that they followed their natural inclination to care for each other.

The traditional American rural community, small town or even large city neighborhood used to be a buttress against individualism run rampant. This is no longer true. The modern economic system was based on individualism. Adam Smith believed that the individual pursuing his or her own self interest even with greedy or selfish motives would ultimately benefit society because the free market would regulate a class of self interests with benefit to all. Whatever truth there may have been to that notion seems to have vanished with the Twenty-first Century economic realities.

"Where there is no vision, the people perish." True enough, but in the United States we have confused the real biblical vision with the alternate notion that the world revolves around the individual whose interests and needs are paramount and take priority over all other considerations. Freedom no longer means that Christ has set us free to contend with the power of sin, but has been reduced to mean that we may now each pursue our own personal goals. Constraints upon individualism run rampant are no longer the common good, but the collision with other selves in the competition of the free market. This kind of thinking has invaded our self-understanding at the deepest levels.

As a demonstration of this, McKibben's article is helpful. He points out that three out of four Americans believe the Bible teaches: "God helps those who help themselves." Actually this bit of wisdom is not found in Scripture. It goes against everything we know of Scripture. It comes from Aesop's Fables and entered American life through Benjamin Franklin's *Poor Richard's Almanack* in 1736. Franklin's aphorism has formed a bedrock upon which we not only operate, but upon which our religious faith rests to a much greater extent than we are willing to recognize.

It is this kind of thinking, not Scripture, that underlies and supports the economic and political institutions in which we live and work. We may try to live our personal lives as Christians and we might be able to pull it off at church, in small groups, and with family, friends and neighbors. But when we leave these small groups, we enter a world of totalitarian consumerism, relentless materialism, narcissistic individualism, unbridled greed and the fascination with power.

The Imperial Self and Civil Religion

The same kind of thinking which leads to the "Imperial Self," when applied to the nation itself becomes a "civil religion". Every nation has some sort of civil religion, but ours, derived from our British ancestors, is somewhat unique in that it applies the Old Testament scriptures to our political system. Since 1630 with John Winthrop's famous "City on the Hill" sermon in Boston, Americans have believed that the biblical imagery of the New Jerusalem, the City on the Hill, the Chosen People applies to us first as British colonists then as citizens of a new nation. That nation, we have always believed, is doing God's work. We are pre-eminent and our enemies are God's enemies.

Now we are the world's lone superpower with no one strong enough to hold us in check. Now we are engaged in a war we need not have begun. Now it's time to rethink very seriously these long held assumptions.

Neither our nation, nor our communities nor our individual selves can survive the rampages of unchecked individualism. It may have gotten us by in the past, but the forces turned loose in the Twenty-first Century will not allow for it to continue.

What we face is not simply an American problem. It affects every part of the planet in one way or another. Forty years ago, I had a conversation with some other Christian missionaries who had gone, as I had done, to live in Japan to proclaim the Gospel in that lovely land. We were discussing how we could live our faith among the Japanese and how to formulate our message to impact that culture, which historically has been almost completely impervious to Christianity. An old German missionary who had been there for many years told us that there was a larger problem than how to proclaim the Gospel in the Japanese culture. "Consider instead," he said, "how we can articulate the Gospel in the technological civilization that is destroying all the world's cultures."

He was correct. Technology added the final straw to the new vision. When science is applied through technological innovation, the number of workers required to produce things drops with increasing orders of magnitude. Reliability and efficiency becomes the only acceptable standards. Competition between individuals for a piece of the action becomes the only rule of the game. Technological civilization, based on the premises operative since the Seventeenth Century, has begun to change significantly all cultures to the point that the society that existed before has been destroyed and something new has taken its place.

We perceive that life is different and the rate of change is accelerating. Workers are interchangeable, replaceable and able to be discarded on a global scale.

Science and technology have diminished the importance of the individual in the world. In the same way, governments have lost some of their sovereign powers in favor of transnational corporations. Vast sums of capital flow from place to place with the speed of electronic transfer. It is now possible to move money so rapidly and in such great quantities that economies can be immediately destabilized.

As we have detached ourselves from the needs of the community, radical individualism, relentless consumerism, crass materialism have become the norm. Competition is now a way of life. Corruption, deceit and manipulation are now standard practice in many places. The chickens hatched so long ago have finally come home to roost.

It Doesn't Have To Be This Way

Fortunately, none of this is irreversible. We cannot and we should not want to turn back the clock. There are tremendous benefits to living in the global society we now inhabit. But we must make this emerging society work better for individuals, families and for smaller communities. The global society, built upon the assumptions I have briefly described, is a product of the "modern" era. This begins roughly in the Seventeenth Century, but in the Twentieth Century, a set of new ideas began to take root. Some say we are now beginning to live in a "postmodern" era. Whatever you choose to call the present age, some new thinking is afoot and Christians have some new tools to use in living our faith. There are some new ways to reconfigure how we live and what we do. They're new ways because they use old principles of community, new kinds of grouping and new technology.

This is actually a moment ripe with immense opportunities for choosing new directions in our culture. New visions are emerging and we are re-examining many of our traditions and social assumptions. The truth about the "postmodern" era is that we have been liberated from some "modern" blind spots and we are now able to take a fresh look at our foundations. The need for moral and religious renewal is obvious. With God's grace and our cooperation it will occur.

For Christians, the opportunity is enormous. We are returning to Scripture and to some very ancient ways of living the faith in order to reformulate them. As Christian people have done often in the past, we are examining the Bible and our Christian history with a fresh approach. We know that God's action among us is not limited to the past, but God is contemporary with us in all generations. With a biblical vision, the people cannot perish.

We were called by God into a community of believers-the Church with Christ as its head. The Church is called to be the witness of Jesus Christ to the world. The Church is called to proclaim the Gospel by word and deed. Paul calls the Church the Body of Christ. The Church is before all else a community. The rest of this book, intended as an antidote to unbridled individualism, will be about how we first envision and then how we can give form and shape to a community life given to us by God in Christ. We will do this by going back to the sources, taking special note of Augustine, the great Christian thinker of the early Church who referred to God as "Beauty ever ancient, ever new." Our life with God, based on the ancient faith, is always "ever new." We begin that search with a passage from Scripture that describes the first Christian community.

"All who believed were together and had all things in common; they would sell their possessions and goods and distribute the proceeds to all, as any had need. Day by day, as they spent much time together in the temple, they broke bread at home and ate their food with glad and generous hearts, praising God and having the goodwill of all the people." (Acts 2: 44-47).

our common life

Two

It's Always Christmas

One evening, when our oldest child was an infant, my wife had been nursing him. As she moved him for a burp, she held him up and said to me: "God became one of these." She was right. At the heart of our Christian faith is the exhilarating belief that the Eternal Word of God, in whose image all things were created, (John 1 & Col 1) entered into creation itself as a helpless infant who was in need of feeding, burping, cleaning and changing. The story of the birth of Jesus in Luke's Gospel never loses its appeal because it tells of God's own Son becoming a helpless child. The Christmas story is always true and its implications for us are endless. So, for Christians, it's always Christmas.

The Christmas story presented a fascinating word play to Augustine and he used it to the maximum extent. Our English word "infant" comes from a Latin word, *fari* which means "to speak." The prefix "in" placed in front of the word negates it. So, an infant (*infans* in Latin) is quite literally and descriptively "one who is unable to speak." There is a very full-throated, powerful and majestic Latin word which is used in John's Gospel to name the Eternal Word of God: *Verbum*. It is used three times in the first sentence of that Gospel. Augustine, whose native language was Latin, loved to juxtapose the big word and the little word to explain that Jesus is fully divine yet fully human: "*Verbum infans*", the speechless Word of God," or "the Word of God, speechless for us."

The implications for us are dramatic. God is both totally and utterly transcendent, beyond us, and beyond the entire vast universe, in ways we simply cannot grasp. Yet God has reached us, not only by revelation, but by physically joining us in that universal human experience of birth. As a speechless, helpless infant. God is still totally beyond us, totally other than we are, but God is now also totally one with us. Christians call this the "Incarnation," a Latin word which means "to become flesh." As John's Gospel tells us "the Word became flesh and lived among us."

God shares a common life with us so total that it begins with conception and birth. The life of God with us also ends in the universal experience of suffering and death. Because of this, our Christian faith can never be a "pie in the sky" kind of religious belief. It is always very messy and earthy. God became accessible to us in the most physically possible way-through birth, life among us and death. This means that our life with God is always rooted in the physical world. God came among us so that the entire human family might share in the blessing first of earthly and then eternal life. Humanity is a single species, so the Incarnation of God in Christ is an invitation to the entire human family both individually and collectively to share in this common life.

This is the great Christian paradox. God is always totally transcendent to us humans and to the entire universe, yet, at the same time God is also one with us as a member of the human family. Our common life together is always founded in this great truth. The paradox begins with the baby Jesus, who is both the Eternal Word of God and a speechless, helpless infant. All Christian activity, including our common life together is firmly rooted in this foundational fact.

Downsizing God

Augustine, realizing that we can only have an incomplete and partial grasp of what this really means, used poetry to come as close as he could to explaining it. Let's begin unfolding a practical Augustinian spirituality with a reflection from Augustine himself on the beauty and the paradox of the common life that God has created with us. It is from a Christmas sermon: Read and enjoy, then reflect a moment.

A manger for his bed,
He holds the world in his hand.

Fed at his mother's breast,
 He is the bread of angels.

Wrapped in swaddling clothes,
 He robes us in endless life.

Nursed by his mother,
 He is adored as God.

Finding no room at the inn,
 He builds his temple in faithful hearts.

43

To make the weak strong,
The strong becomes weak.[1]

Notice that there is a purpose to this "downsizing" of God. It takes place to make the weak strong and to build a temple in faithful hearts. God chooses to dwell intimately with us in our humanity, not just as a member of our race, but also even at the center of each individual's heart in a deeply personal way. The Creator of the cosmos seeks an intimate relationship with each of us. Augustine builds on this: Christ is in no way diminished by his smallness, nor is he demeaned by the earthiness of his surroundings. Even more than that, Christ's emptiness is our fullness. Ultimately the weakness of Christ leads to his death, which becomes the source of our eternal life.

Augustine puts it this way:

Christ's feebleness is our firmness, Christ's infant inability to talk is our eloquence, Christ's need is our abundance, because later Christ's death also became our life.[2]

In a culture that demands efficiency, perfection and prizes strength, loves "winners" and despises "losers," we need to take to heart the fact that it is the grace and power of God which sustains our own feeble efforts. St. Paul discovered this the hard way when he was confronted with his own frailty, the "thorn in the flesh" whatever that may have been. Having asked God to remove it from him, the answer came and Paul understood it: "My grace is sufficient for you, for my power is made perfect in weakness." (2 Cor 12:9). Only then was Paul able to "boast of my weakness so that Christ's power may rest

on me." Common life requires that we have a realistic assess-
ment of ourselves and of other people. God comes to us at
the very center of our weakness. We no longer need to pos-
ture and pretend to be what we are not. As a friend once told
me, "being God is not part of my job description." When we
understand this, the spiritual life takes on a new meaning and
community becomes more desirable.

Augustine ties together the Christmas theme by contrasting
the infant's greatness in the form of God with his smallness in
the form of a servant.

Creator of heaven and earth,
He was born on earth under heaven.
Unspeakably wise, he is wisely speechless.
Filling the world, he lies in a manger.
Ruler of the stars, he nurses at his mother's breast.
He is both great in the nature of God
and small in the form of a servant,
but in such way that his greatness
is not diminished by his smallness,
nor his smallness overwhelmed by his greatness.[3]

The infant Word of God is both great in the nature of God
and small in the form of the servant. This is not original with
Augustine. It is derived directly from the earliest Christian
hymn, which Paul either composed himself or heard sung in
the Church but which he included in the Letter to the
Philippians. This is a central New Testament passage.

[5] Let the same mind be in you that was in Christ Jesus,
[6] who, though he was in the form of God,

did not regard equality with God
as something to be exploited,
[7] but emptied himself,
taking the form of a slave,
being born in human likeness.
And being found in human form,
[8]   he humbled himself
and became obedient to the point of death-
even death on a cross.
[9] Therefore God also highly exalted him
and gave him the name
that is above every name,
[10] so that at the name of Jesus
every knee should bend,
in heaven and on earth and under the earth,
[11] and every tongue should confess
that Jesus Christ is Lord,
to the glory of God the Father. (Phil 2: 5-11)

The first part of the hymn is about the "emptying" of God in Christ. Though fully God and Lord, Jesus emptied himself to the point of taking on the form of a slave. Slaves in the ancient world could be executed by their owners. This self-emptying went even so far as the disgraceful death of a convicted criminal on the cross, a terrible instrument of torture used by the Romans to terrorize subject peoples.

The second part shows the result of this self-emptying. God exalts the crucified slave, the Word made flesh. In the ancient world if you knew a person's name, you knew the person, so names had a tremendous significance in that era. The name given to Jesus is Lord. It is the same name given to God. The slave who was executed as a criminal by the lords and rulers of the world is revealed as the Lord of all and worthy of our worship. Every knee should bend and confess that he is Lord.

Nowhere else in Scripture is the paradox of our Christian faith contained more clearly and succinctly. It contains our marching orders as well. The first words of the passage spell out what we are to do. We are told: "Have that mind in you which was in Christ Jesus...." We are to have the same kind of attitude that was found in Jesus. As he was willing to empty himself from the vantage point even of the nature of God, then we, creatures must have this same kind of mind toward our fellow humans that was found in him. This is our call to love and serve others. It is a call to action. It is the foundation of our common life together. As we allow ourselves to be shaped and formed by God who calls us to this kind of love and service, we begin to live in real community.

Common Life Begins With God

Scripture tells us that our primary relationship is with God and that is where our common life begins. All of our other relationships echo the nature and quality of this first, primary one. In Matthew, we read:

"But when the Pharisees heard that he had silenced the Sadducees, they came together. And one of them, a lawyer, asked him a question, to test him. "Teacher, which is the great commandment in the law?" And he said to him, "You shall love the Lord your God with all your heart, and with all your soul, and with all your mind. This is the great and first commandment. And a second is like it, you shall love your neigh-

47

bor as yourself. On these two commandments depend all the law and the prophets." (Mt. 22:23-40)

How do we relate to God? Our relationship with God is not like any other. We cannot grasp God through our five senses, nor can we really understand the divine presence. It is almost as if God is lurking at the horizon of human consciousness in a most mysterious way-as a personal presence and yet beyond our capacity to really comprehend. Scripture is very clear that God is a personal being and not just a force-and this corresponds with our own religious experience.

A bishop, preacher and writer, Augustine spoke and wrote about God incessantly. Yet, when all is said and done, when we have prayed, reflected on Scripture, read whatever we can, we know more what God is not than what God is. God is ultimately incomprehensible to us. Our minds are incapable of really grasping the One who created "the vast expanse of interstellar space." Augustine remarks: "if you can understand something, it is not God."[4]

For Augustine, we know God primarily through love. In fact love is at the root of all knowledge and motivation: "my weight is my love, it takes me wherever I may go." But we cannot love what we don't know. We know God inwardly, but only in a hidden and partial way, but we can't do even this without God's help:

"I entered into my inmost parts with you leading me on. I was able to do it because you had become my helper."[6]

Augustine thinks that personal desire and a hunger for something or someone is what drives us in everything we do.[7] So we seek God, not just to believe, but also, if possible, to experience something of God. He quotes the Psalmist, who compares our longing for God with the longing of a deer for streams of water. (Ps. 42: 1)

It is important to grasp this in our culture where love and desire have been trivialized and knowledge is seen more as information-often with a technical or business slant. We need to reexamine in some depth what our Christian tradition offers. The distinction between feeling and thinking has diminished and assertions have taken the place of thoughtful opinions. Religious thought and language has taken on the cast of the culture and we are all poorer for it.

There are two crucial ways that God is present to us. At first they seem to be totally opposed to each other, but they really are not. Paradoxically, the journey toward community begins with a turn to the deepest regions of our inner self. The inward search confirms the truth that God is both intimately present to us and yet totally beyond us. Again, let Augustine be our guide. Speaking to God in prayer, he writes:

"For you were more inward to me than the most inward part of me and higher than my highest reach."[8]

So God is both more intimate to us than we are to ourselves and at the same time further beyond us than even the cosmos itself. This is not some kind of "new age" notion that the universe is all just one great force and we are all part of it. Quite the contrary, it restates dramatically the Christian belief that

God, the Creator of the cosmos, entered the human race in Jesus. Here Augustine goes even further, emphasizing that God "abides in us, by the Spirit that he has given us." (1 Jn: 3: 24). On the night before he died, Jesus promised to send the Spirit to his disciples. (Jn 14:26). The New Testament is filled with references to the Holy Spirit coming to us. This single sentence of Augustine encapsulates a vast amount of biblical material. The insight that God is more inward to him than he is to himself, allows Augustine to reflect on this entire teaching and then utter it in the form of a prayer from the depths of his soul.

The God who is totally transcendent to us is also so intimate as to be grasped as abiding within us. This is bedrock traditional Christian spirituality. If we start seeking God and not ourselves, then we will find God and discover how enriched we are by God's presence. If we begin seeking ourselves, then we end up only with our limited and broken selves.

Finding God after a long detour through the various philosophies and worldview of his time, Augustine writes:

"Late have I loved you, O Beauty so ancient and so new; late have I loved you. For behold you were within me, and I outside."[9]

In an even more radical step, he affirms that it is by knowing ourselves that we can know God more deeply.

"Pray in the most brief and perfect way possible: 'O God, always the same, let me know myself, let me know you.' That's the prayer."[10]

Look again at the Christmas poems and you will see that Augustine combines both aspects of God in single sentences and tries to place them within our reach: Example: "Creator of heaven and earth, He was born on earth under heaven." And "Unspeakably wise, he is wisely speechless." Again: "Filling the world, he lies in a manger" And "Ruler of the stars, he nurses at his mother's breast." God is always with us as totally transcendent and totally intimate.

For Augustine, the very heart of community with God begins with a grasp of the two modes of God's presence. Of course, this is not original with him, for it is most clearly expressed in the "hymn" we quoted from Paul's letter to the Philippians.

The first part of the hymn is about the "descent" of the Eternal Word of God. The one who is "by nature God," not only "emptied himself" being found in human form and born in human likeness, but even further, "he humbled himself" to the point even of death on a cross as a disgraced criminal. God's relationship with us is not just one of self-emptying, but even further of humility. It is truly breathtaking that the Creator of the World becomes humbled before sinful creatures. This is how God initiates a common life with us. Here, God is coming "toward" us in the person of Jesus. We call this mode of God's presence *kataphatic*, from the Greek word *kata*, which means "near" or "toward."

The second part of the hymn in Philippians is about the ascent of the risen Christ, still physical and fully human, but now beyond the limitations of suffering and death, into that place which is his by right. The concluding line of the hymn

51

leaves no doubt that Jesus Christ has the name that is above all names and is Lord. This mode of presence is called *apophatic*, from the Greek *apo*, which means "away from" or "distant."

These two opposite poles of God's presence to us are both richly described in Scripture. Some passages depict God as coming toward us. Others portray God as being very distant and completely beyond us. The first creation story in Genesis (Gen 1:1-2:4) depicts God as serenely above everything creating the world. In the second creation story (Gen 2:4-24) God is pictured at work in the Garden fashioning the man and the woman out of the dust of earth. In the first story God transcends the universe. In the second story God is actively at work inside the world (the appropriate word is "immanent").

In the Exodus story, God calls Moses from the burning bush and Moses is truly frightened by this awesome presence. When he finally dares to ask God's name, he is simply told: "I am who I am." The message is clear: God is above and beyond all names. But soon, God engages in real dialogue with Moses and works within the world to free the people from slavery in Egypt. Moses experiences both modes of God's presence.

In the New Testament, God comes among us and towards us in a most appealing way, as an infant. The infant grown into adulthood walks the roads of his homeland, goes to parties, talks to people. His friends and followers converse with him, eat and drink with him and finally he dies among them. These stories depict God as coming towards us, being immanent within the world and being intimate with us.

In other stories, especially the resurrection narratives, the risen

Lord is clearly distant and transcendent. He has gone beyond death and into new life. Thomas does not dare to accept the Lord's invitation to put his hands in the marks of the wounds, but simply replies "My Lord and my God." (Jn 20:28)When Mary Magdalene finally recognizes the risen Jesus, he tells her "do not hold on to me...." (Jn 20:17)

At first glance, all this might seem abstract, but it is not. On the contrary, it is very practical. It has tremendous significance in our own personal spiritual life. At some times God seems intimate and we feel like praying with an outpouring of words and even with some enthusiasm. Our spiritual life seems to be going fine. At other times God seems very distant and we can find no words for prayer. At some times we feel blessed and comforted by God; at others, God seems absent. Often people become very upset because they no longer feel God's intimate presence. There's really nothing wrong with that-it is simply the personal experience of God's distance from us. Our personal spirituality must combine both the *kataphatic* and *apophatic.* Without the first, God would be inaccessible and we would never pray. Without the second, we would become too glib and forget that this is really God, the creator of the universe with whom we have a personal relationship.

Common life viewed through the prism of Augustinian spirituality requires first that we be "saturated in Scripture." This does not mean just Bible study alone, but Bible study with some knowledge of the historical context in which Scripture was written. It also requires that we have some knowledge of the way our Christian ancestors throughout the ages have interpreted and lived their faith. Classic Christian history and theology has much to offer us.

Two Metaphors: The spiritual night and the cloud of unknowing

Regarding the two modes of God's presence, we American Christians tend mostly toward the *kataphatic*. We want a God we can know clearly and distinctly and yet we know in our hearts that God is beyond our comprehension. We want to know God's purpose for us and feel secure in the knowledge that we are fulfilling this purpose, but we dwell in ambivalence and uncertainty. We need to realize that this problem has been faced before, not only by Augustine, but by countless others down through the ages. Awareness of the *apophatic* realm is a corrective to the "big guy in the sky" illusion that God is just a bigger, better version of ourselves.

Two metaphors are helpful, both by authors who knew Augustine well. The first describes this as a spiritual "dark night" and even describes stages. The first part of the night resembles twilight, when sensible objects begin to fade from view. This is the period when we begin to anticipate the suffering of the cross. The second part of the night is the very darkness of midnight as we stand at the foot of the cross and experience something of the suffering of Jesus. We do not at this time see the light. We walk during this time of bleakness purely by faith. We know that dawn will come but we see no evidence of it. The third part of the night is that before first light. The dawn has not yet arrived, but we can distinguish the terrain once again. We actually are living in the light during this part of the night. This is the first Easter glimpse of the risen

54

Lord.[11]

The second helpful metaphor is that of "the cloud of unknowing." Some of our contemporaries seem to think they have a pipeline to the divine mind. They are absolutely certain of God's intentions, be it to invade Iraq, to steer society in a particular direction, to introduce economic change, or whatever. Assertions proclaimed publicly and loudly with unqualified certainty and with disdain for those who disagree have done much to rupture the fabric of our life together. Our public discourse has degenerated into a shouting match, with competing certainties hurled back and forth.

It is helpful to know that through the ages men and women have been content with a more modest grasp of God. The "cloud" metaphor is an *apophatic* corrective to this war of certainties. The truly wise are aware of how little they really know. In discerning the mind of God, we know very little indeed. This "cloud" is nothing more than an up-close demonstration given by God of the vast gulf that lies between God and humanity. "My thoughts are not your thoughts, neither are your ways my ways." (Is.55:8)

The "cloud" experience teaches us how little we really understand God. It resembles driving through a thick and impenetrable fog or low cloud. Anyone who has ever driven under these conditions knows that you must slow down and sometimes even stop. The same is true in the spiritual journey. It teaches us to trust God even though we do not and cannot know Him now face to face. We do not now know how it is that his justice and mercy will be finally vindicated, but we trust that it will. The "cloud" is a very deep and personal intuition of this. We must learn to "be at home in this darkness."[12]

A deeply personal search for God through these different stages and through the fog of our own ignorance gives the Augustinian way of life its contemplative dimension. This is the spiritual root and foundation from which activity flows. In our growing awareness of God, we become attentive to whom we really are. We neither diminish our self-worth nor exaggerate it. We become more at peace with ourselves and with God. This is genuine humility, a necessity for the Christian life. We see that our own sin, frailty, ignorance-the broken places of our lives-are redeemed by God's graceful presence.

Genuine humility allows us to be at home with ourselves and to form a loving community with our fellow sinners. Luke's Gospel records that two men went up to the temple to pray. One thanked God that he was not like the rest of humanity, especially like the disreputable fellow standing in the back with his eyes cast down. The latter could only pray, "God, be merciful to me, a sinner." Jesus tells us that this man went home justified before God. (Luke 18: 10-14) It is very difficult to forge a real bond with those who fancy themselves above the common herd. Real community is possible only if it is rooted in genuine humility.

How to Begin

Augustinian common life begins with God and extends outward to others through genuine encounters at the deepest levels of our spiritual selves. With this in mind, I suggest that readers begin to seek out others in their churches, at work, in other religious traditions, in neighborhoods or wherever, and form groups in which this kind of mutual exchange can take place. This should at some point entail serious Bible study, theological discussion, sharing of joys and blessings, problems and obstacles. This kind of grouping can be so significant as to be life changing. It is also a very appealing form of spiritual formation and preparation for the next steps outward to form community with the wider world.

I suggest that people of different Christian traditions worship together at each others churches. Because the revelation of God in Christ is so large, each of our groups has only a limited grasp of the great reality.

Interestingly, Evangelical piety tends towards the *kataphatic* with emphasis on the kind of personal relationship with Jesus that implies easy intimacy: the language used indicates this; dialogical prayer, easy familiarity, emphasis on happiness, feeling, emotion.

Catholic, Eastern Orthodox and Anglican sacramental piety tends towards the *apophatic*. The presence of Christ in the sacraments implies the "larger" transcendent presence of the post resurrection Lord. We are "drawn into" the sacramental presence. Words are seen as inadequate expressions. The total person, body and all the senses are involved in worship.

As I have said, both facets of the spiritual life are biblical, both are essential and we each need to cultivate both sides of our spiritual life. In this way too, the circle of our community grows ever larger. This is a further step in our mission to the world community.

We began this chapter with Augustine's Christmas poems because the Christmas story is a delightful place to begin our long spiritual journey. We then travel with Jesus through the years of his ministry, listening to his teaching, learning of his deeds. We end up at the foot of the cross, sharing the desolation of that awful place. We incorporate the meaning of suffering and death into our own spiritual lives and we experience the first light of the resurrection even in that darkness. But the journey does not end here. There is an even more breathtaking climax in store for us. Scripture reveals a destiny for the human community beyond our wildest dreams.

The early church writers, including Augustine, were fascinated by the statement in Genesis that humanity was created in the image and likeness of God. (Gen 1:26). The New Testament reveals to us the one God as Father, Son and Holy Spirit. We understand that God being one in nature is also, in ways we cannot grasp, also a community of persons. We refer to God in this way as a Trinity of persons. The very nature of this one God is to exist in a perfect community of love among Father, Son and Holy Spirit.

Scripture reveals to us that we, made in the image and likeness of God, are also called to be "partakers of the divine nature." (2 Peter 1:4) This does not mean, of course, that we become God, for Christ, the Eternal Word of God is the true, perfect and divine image of God. But our likeness to God allows us in a very limited and partial way to come within the ambit of the community life of God. Paul tells us that "we are children of God, and if children, then heirs, heirs of God and fellow heirs with Christ" (Romans 8:16). We are, through Christ, children of the Father by "adoption." (Eph 1:5; Rom 8: 15, 23,

58

9:4)

This is a very large picture. The ultimate destiny of our human community is to enter in some limited way into the enjoyment of the common life between Father, Son and Holy Spirit. One of Augustine's greatest books is *On the Trinity*. He believed that within the inmost structures of the person seeking God, there is not only a glimpse of our likeness to God, but there is also a faint awareness that our inner selves are configured to the Trinity as well.[13]

Augustine's tendency to search within himself has not the slightest hint of the kind of spiritual narcissism we find today. Nor is there any room for a "just me and Jesus" approach. If our inner awareness leads us to a hint of the abiding presence of the Trinity, then we perceive that we are created for relationships. If we are engulfed somehow within the love that exists among the Father, Son and Holy Spirit, we also perceive that we, made in the image of God, are created to love others.

As the Word of God became in our behalf a speechless, helpless infant, we, still speechless, helpless and in darkness before the greatness of God, are yet called into a share in the eloquence, power and brightness of the common life of God. At the end of the journey, the Christmas poem is fulfilled completely: "To make the weak strong, the strong becomes weak." It follows then, that we, being made strong by him, now engage others to share that strength with them.

We cannot begin to consider our common life together from an Augustinian perspective unless we realize the vast sweep of our Christian faith all the way from its humblest beginnings to its transcendent destiny. Nor can we form communities able to confront the hyper-individualism and narcissism of our culture in any effective way unless we are deeply grounded in our faith. We must allow ourselves to be drawn along at every step of the way by the grace of God who calls to us from the very center of our souls.

We acknowledge to God, as did Augustine: "you were more inward to me than the most inward part of me and higher than my highest reach." We pray again and again, "Let me know myself, let me know you." Such prayer is wellspring of our common life and through it, we allow God to send us out in love and service to others.

I suggest using these prayers, poems and the biblical passages upon which they are based as companions on the journey. Etch them in your "deep memory" by prayerful repetition, for there they are immediately accessible as a basis for action.

Three

The Restless Heart

The house was large and impressive, the furnishings beautiful and the setting almost idyllic in the lake country of northern New Jersey. The snow was fresh and it was very cold. The ice on the lake would be perfect for the skating party we had planned for the evening. College students on winter break from school, we had nothing on our minds but fun.

My date for the evening was the daughter of the house, a very attractive young woman I had met only the day before. Raised in Southern California, I had never been on ice skates, but was convinced that it was the same as roller skating, so I looked forward to impressing my date with my sunbelt skating skills.

The only obstacle to the evening's enjoyment was the girl's father, who insisted on making conversation with me while I waited for his daughter to come downstairs. We began what I thought would be the usual strained-conversation-with-girl's-father while I was waiting for my date. I remarked that he had a nice house. He agreed, but then said, "It wasn't worth it." I looked puzzled so he began to open his soul to a nineteen-year-old college student he'd never seen before.

My date's father was a vice president in a large New York corporation. He had everything he'd ever wanted but somehow his life was empty. Neither marriage and family nor job nor social and political connections had brought him the happiness he had expected when he began his career. His daughter's arrival ended the conversation.

I discovered that ice-skating isn't the same as roller skating. I spent the evening in a sitting position on the ice much to the amusement of my date and her friends. The girl was not impressed and I never saw her again, but I never forgot the conversation with her father.

Her father was right. Even great success never fully satisfies. A certain flatness and even emptiness of soul often sets in soon after achievement. Realization slowly dawns that life cannot be completely fulfilling. We do not accept this notion easily.

Perhaps we begin with unrealistic expectations or we hope for too much from life. Nor is our desire merely for material success. We seek also the esteem and affection of others, psychological/spiritual fulfillment and a kind of general sense of well being.

But all satisfaction is incomplete and fleeting. Are we ever loved enough? Do our children develop according to our expectations? What job or profession leaves us completely fulfilled? When is friendship or marriage perfect? When does lovemaking leave us satisfied beyond anticipation of the next time? Incompleteness lies at the heart of all experience.

We are finite, limited creatures possessed of an unlimited, infi-

nite capacity for fulfillment. Even when we are largely satisfied, new yearnings arise almost immediately. The process is
endless, quieted only by the final un-fulfillment of death.

Augustine locates the source of this frustrated yearning within the human heart in one of the great "one-liners" of all time.
"You have made us for yourself, O Lord, and our heart is restless until it rests in you."[14]

The Restless Heart

According to Augustine, the endlessly-unfulfilled search has a
purpose. It points us in the right direction, the only direction
in which we will find complete fulfillment.

We seek our own happiness above all else, but the more experience we have in life, the more we come to understand that
nothing-people, possessions, personal well-being-brings us
perfect happiness. The never-ending search for happiness
never brings more than partial fulfillment. We always crave
more. The inner restlessness only increases as we grow older.
This is true no matter how satisfied we are with our lives.

We are creatures dependent upon God for existence. Because
we are not self-sufficient, we continue to experience our own
radical insufficiency in all that we do and all that we seek. Our
inner restlessness torments us and will not allow us to stop
short of God who alone is capable of fulfilling us completely.[15]

Augustine believed that the restless heart was absolutely essential because we must first experience our finiteness in every

area of our being before we can come to grips with God. This means that we cannot in principle be spiritually satisfied by anything, even by our own religious experience. Life's searching ends only when we have reached our final destiny of eternal "face to face" common life with God.

Our restless heart is indispensable. It is a motivation to seek God that is embedded within us-a crucial component of our human "hardware." It's a built-in magnet that attracts us to God. Paul tells us that God desires the salvation of all people (1 Tim 2:4; 4:10). All humanity, he insists, has a basic understanding of God and his law written on the heart. (Rom 2:12-16).

God is the object of the search, the object of all human striving. God uses our own restlessness, our ceaseless yearning as a means to draw us toward that ultimate fulfillment when we shall see "face to face and be known even as we are known." (1 Cor 13:12) We need not be consciously aware of God. Our restlessness is so pervasive and profound that we are drawn toward God even though we are ignorant of whom we seek. In all our struggles for fulfillment and happiness we come to realize that we have been seeking God all along.[16] At the deepest levels of the spirit, the restless heart moves us on beyond restlessness to a place of inner stillness where we abide in the "peace that passes all understanding."(Phil 4:7) Daily life with all its usual turbulence continues, but there is a growing peace deep within us which remains unshaken.

If we are firmly convinced that God alone can fill our deepest longing, we will not expect anyone or anything else to calm our restlessness. While still striving for goals in life, we will be able

64

to bask joyfully in the presence of family and friends and to enjoy what we have without constantly churning inwardly for more and more and more of whatever we want at the moment. It is now possible to take the first steps out of a frenetic consumer-driven life style and perhaps even to slow down the rat-race. The restless heart allows us, quite paradoxically, to make decisions from a place of deep peace.

The Restless Heart and Pilgrim People

Restless hearts are also more open to the possibilities of change. Our market-driven global society generates massive upheavals with the flow of jobs and money around the world. Even where there is no physical displacement, it seems often that the entire culture is undergoing a seismic shift. The restless heart, having its final home in God, is less reluctant to be "on the move" than someone whose entire energy is consumed in maintaining the status quo.

Being on the move is quite biblical. God called Abraham out of Haran and sent him to Canaan. Abraham's descendants were always on the move: into Egypt and out of Egypt, wandering through the desert, finding their land, into exile, and then returning.

The New Testament people were also on the move. From the upper room at Pentecost, they went first to their own countrymen, then to "all the nations", as Jesus commanded them. Paul was the most well-known of many "wandering apostles" who took the Gospel to the edges of the known world.

Members of the early Church were aware that they were a "pilgrim people". When they proclaimed "Jesus is Lord," that meant that Caesar was not. This got them in a lot of trouble. During the first three centuries, thousands were killed for their faith and many others were dispersed. In their sufferings and in their journeys they were rooted in faith. Their restless hearts were grounded always in God. Their fellow citizens saw how they lived and were attracted to them. Eventually the Roman Empire collapsed, but the Church endured.

The migrations of the early Church were not only physical, but cultural as well. The small group of Jewish disciples immediately began to include the vastly larger Gentile population. For that reason, the New Testament was written in Greek, the common language of the time, and the early disciples formulated their message using terms that Greeks and Romans could understand. At every step of the journey, they assimilated the language and customs of the cultures in which they lived, rooting them firmly in the faith. They knew their destiny was always ahead of them. No matter how widely they were persecuted, the risen Christ awaited them at the "end of the age". They always knew who it was in whom their hearts would rest.

When the persecutions ended, the emperor Constantine made Christianity the religion of the Empire. Many Christians grew complacent and comfortable and this created a different kind of restlessness within the Church. Not wanting to grow flabby in the faith, a few wandered into the deserts and isolated places to focus more intently on God. Others joined these "hermits," and bands settled in one place and became monks. People flocked to them because they esteemed their spiritual depth. Hospitality to visitors was a key point of monastic life. Benedict, the great founder of western monasticism stated in his rule that every guest should be treated as if that person were Christ. Monasteries had a tremendous impact upon the way the faith was lived throughout both eastern and western Europe.

As time went on, widespread restlessness set in again. Monasteries had become comfortable and complacent. New economic and political systems began to emerge. People were once again on the move. Wandering bands of "hermits" sprang up and there were "pilgrims" going to various places. Clearly something new was needed to meet the spiritual needs of a newly-restless people.

During the Thirteenth Century, new kinds of religious orders sprang up. Their focus was to serve the needs of the people who were moving into new places and new ways of living in new political and economic systems. Stable monastic communities were still necessary. But these new groups were to be on the move with the people. They were to go with the people, not only from place to place, but into the marketplaces and the universities that were emerging. The Augustinians were one such group.

From the Thirteenth Century when it was founded, Augustinian spirituality has been filtered through this lens of high mobility. St. Augustine may have wanted a stable and set-tled monastic community, but he himself, though he ended up staying a long time in one place, lived a busy and untradition-al monastic life.

The task faced by Augustinians for the last seven hundred years and more has been to incorporate the spiritual life of Augustine into a deliberately restless mode of living.

Augustinians are not monks, but they are supposed to be as spiritually focused and prayerful as monks. The chapel with its regular hours for prayer is the center of monastic life, but the chapel is not central for Augustinians. The common life itself and the "common room" where they gather is the center for them. Augustinian prayer life must be as intentional and focused as it is for monks, but it is prayer "on the move."

The Twenty-first Century began with an expectation of constant and rapid change. To use computer language, it seems we are now hardwired for ever accelerating rates of change. This creates a kind of restlessness that is often pathological and destructive. Job changes, military deployment, displacement, job loss, cities in which there is no real community-places where one can be lonely while surrounded by thousands of people-these are the hallmarks of our era. Confusing change, relentless pressure, growing uncertainty about the future: these are things that become increasingly familiar to us.

The Challenge for Today

Living out an Augustinian approach to the Christian life today means jumping right into this boiling cauldron with the clear intention of redirecting the restlessness toward God. Jesus sent the first disciples out "two by two," on the first missionary journey, (Mk 6:6;Lk 10:1) so no one should attempt to do this alone. Jesus promised us, "wherever two or three are gathered in my name, there am I in the midst of them." (Mt. 18:19) Common life in some depth and a serious prayer focus, such as I have outlined, are prerequisites for any Christian venture, but are absolutely indispensable for an undertaking like this.

The Bishop of Hippo laid a spiritual groundwork in the late Fourth and early Fifth Centuries for a specific way of understanding and living the Christian life. That groundwork proved to be enduring and powerful. It was redirected and channeled in a new direction in the thirteenth century. This channel has itself proven to be a conduit of grace for countless people.

Augustinians have begun to search for new ways of responding to God's call in our time because it is now clear that another redirection is required. The rest of this book will consist of my suggestions on how the newly restless people of God might form a "common life on the move and in the street." The Augustinian way of life is like a surfboard: it enables you to ride the restless waves gracefully and beautifully to a specific place on the shore. We'll be discussing some of the moves to make on the way into the beach.

our common life

Four

Community: In the Rough and On the Run

In the Army, we learned that to march in formation meant we had to step out with our left foot when we heard the command "Forward, march." To learn to live in community, we must start by plunging our toes (either foot) into the waters of real life. Opportunities will find us. We don't have to go looking for them, but we do have to be very intentional about loving others and about forming community. We can begin with some simple ways of practicing common life "in the rough and on the run".

There is a radical element in Augustine's idea of common life. It all begins with the commandment to love-and this commandment includes everyone. He writes: "There is no member of the human species to whom love is not due...at least because we are united to them as human beings."[17]

Augustine's Rule for his religious community begins with a prologue: "Before all else, dearly beloved brothers, love God and then your neighbor, for these are the principal commandments given to us." For Augustine, love is primarily embodied in friendship and companionship.

The common room in an Augustinian house is the place where the community gathers for recreation. It is a place of companionship and friendship. It is no exaggeration to say that for Augustinians the common room rather than the chapel is the center of life.[18] The common room is not just a room in a building, but it is really wherever we are together. It is also a place of enjoyment and laughter. To transfer elements of this kind of common life beyond the sheltering walls of a religious community requires both a commitment to do it and also some training.

I See Real People

The first step is to recognize that those we meet in any setting, even in the briefest encounters, are real people. Whenever people meet, our faith tells us that the encounter is potentially a sacred event.

It is impossible to have deep friendship with more than a few people. We can have more casual friendships with more, but even then there's a limit simply in terms of time. Fortunately, living in community doesn't require us to exceed those limits or devote every waking moment to making new friends. There is no limit to the number of exercises of friendliness and "kindly companionship" that we can have every day in transitory encounters.

Small steps first. One place to start, as I learned from my wife, is in checkout lines at supermarkets. No matter how hurried or frustrated we might be in from waiting in line for the cashier, we can use the checkout transaction as an occasion to have a real, personal, human connection with the person at the cash register. It might be only a smile or a "thank you," but it can and should be a deliberate attempt to recognize and respect the dignity of that person and the contribution he or she is making to our lives. This is a "mini" form of companionship with another person who is, as God's creation, worthy of respect and affection.

Fast food servers, department store clerks, trades people, garage mechanics, and people waiters in restaurants, hotel maids, janitors, bank tellers: we encounter these and many other ordinary working people on a regular basis. Though we may not know them personally, they are important in our lives. Without them, life as we know it would not exist. We depend upon them, and they upon us. To recognize their role in our lives is simply to acknowledge the truth that we are all linked together, not only as members of the human community, but as co-creators with them of the social system we inhabit. Our life together is a reality-we need to acknowledge their importance to us in a passing moment of grace.

These mundane daily transactions can have enduring consequences. Though we don't reflect on it often, the fact is that the population of the world consists of a single human community. Every person we encounter is a part of that community. Whenever we thoughtfully and intentionally do anything to acknowledge and respect another person's humanity, we enhance our common life together in at least two ways. First, we create an attitude toward this person. This changes our perceptions and our behavior. Second, while the impact of such acts of courtesy on the other person may be unknown, most of the time that person appreciates, acknowledges and responds to an act of courteous kindness. Continued over time, small acts of congeniality bring about habitually gracious behavior.

In a fleeting transaction, lasting only a few seconds, common life is deliberately acknowledged and shared by two strangers. Our life together grows stronger for at least an instant. It doesn't take much imagination to see the impact on the world community if large numbers of people acted this way consistently.

We do not even have to like the people with whom we engage in this kind of common life. They can be rude, obnoxious, nasty people, but if we acknowledge them also as members of our common human family, then we are changed perhaps more deeply than if they were friendly to us. It is also possible that kind and loving behavior might influence them in ways we cannot see. Augustine believes we can even love enemies in this way.[19]

Economic Justice

Augustine ascribes great importance to the fact that the earliest church held all things in common.[20] The common sharing of possessions became for him a bedrock principle. It has been a hallmark of Augustinian spirituality ever since. Many of the transitory encounters I have described involve the exchange of money. In some of these places customer tips are part of the wage calculation. Most employees in such places just get by from paycheck to paycheck. A generous tip is for them more than just a gesture. It helps them to survive.

If we ourselves become employers, hiring gardeners, people to care for our children or construction workers, paying not only a living, but even a generous wage is the way we live out this dimension of our Christian life. Paying the people who work for us a just wage and tipping generously are crucial ways to demonstrate how we follow Christ.

There is a cost to Christian discipleship and that often includes a personal financial cost. Many churches call upon their members to contribute generously even to the point of tithing. Even though pastors seldom preach it from the pulpit, I believe tipping and paying a just wage are equally important. The Bible is very clear about economic justice, practicing hospitality, sharing one's goods and the like. Augustine was also in no doubt about it. My suggestions are simply ways to live out our Christian calling in a very fragmented, fast-paced, individualistic society. These really are small, beginning steps, but crucial if we are to go further.

Kindly Companionship Boot Camp

Army training conditioned us to exceed what we had thought were our limitations. Running in cadence for seemingly-endless periods of time, dropping for countless pushups: it all turned out to be achievable.

Similarly, kindly companionship in the transactions I have described is a good place to begin getting in condition for the "spiritual boot camp" of real community life. At first it seems impossible to operate this way consistently, but over time and with lots of practice, we find that it becomes a way of life. God's love lies at the root of friendship and brings into being all community life. A conscious, intentional and willing response to God's grace is really the only thing required.

Imagine a kindly Drill Instructor who invites you to engage others in loving encounters in every situation. This DI doesn't wear a "Smokey Bear" hat, nor yell and scream, nor demand that you "drop for twenty." Your inner DI helps you in a very gentle way to embody a disciplined kindness toward others.

What begins in checkout lines continues at work. It doesn't matter where you work. The people might be customers, clients, students, patients, competitors or colleagues and co-workers. The principle is the same and the activity is simply an extension of what we have discussed. While maintaining all the appropriate boundaries required in any workplace, the quality and depth of personal relationships at all levels can be transformed by practicing kindly companionship.

I learned a lesson in common life from my first boss when I went to work for what was then called the Veterans Administration, but is now the Department of Veterans Affairs. When I had finished my paperwork at the personnel office, I reported to him. He asked me, "Who do you work for now?" Responding with what I thought was the correct answer, I replied, "The VA." He looked at me and said quite firmly, "No, the VA pays your salary, you work for the veteran."

A few days later, after some training in VA benefits, I found myself sitting at a desk advising veterans and their family members on how to file a claim, gathering information from them about their military service, financial status and the like. Most were easy to deal with, but there was a small but memorable minority who were truly obnoxious and offensive in their attitudes and behavior. My VA training-and my Christian background-reminded me that I was to maintain under all circumstances a helpful and respectful attitude toward even these people. "I understand your problem, Mr. X., but how may I help you?" These were not easy words to say and mean. It was a little like being back in the Army and wishing I were someplace else. I realize now that was indeed a crucial part of my spiritual boot camp.

We all face similar opportunities for growth. We must first recognize them for what they are and then spring into action, drawing on the reflexes we developed during our spiritual basic training.

Many of us have more than one job during our careers. We find ourselves doing a variety of tasks. Most of us have been on both sides of some kind of customer service counter. Teachers have all been students, doctors are also patients, parents used to be children; employees of all kinds have to be themselves customers as well. There is simply no escape from the type of situations I have described. The only question is how do we handle them?

We're In The Same Unit

The Augustinian thread I find running throughout my various careers has been the consistent attempt to establish a common ground with the individuals and the groups with whom I find myself engaged. Using the VA as an example, every individual veteran has specific needs as well as a unique story. Often the story is interesting. As the veteran talks, the true person begins to emerge. It is usually possible to form some kind of a bond

77

and to commit oneself to "walking with" the person through the particular and very specific issue that has brought the person to the office.

During the few minutes together, perhaps filling out a VA claim form, we are in a small and limited way "in the same unit". We are for a few moments "serving together". This is not like being under enemy fire together with the camaraderie that develops in a combat unit, of course, but perhaps the veteran is under fire from financial need or has a disability which requires compensation, or needs medical care. For the time we are together, we are indeed under the kind of economic or social enemy fire that has brought the veteran to the VA. By working together to "accomplish the mission" at hand, we are able to build a bond of affection that is transitory, but very real.

The same kinds of opportunities present themselves to teachers. From my own teaching experience, I know that each class has a unique flavor and spirit with its own unrepeatable blend of student characters. Every class day is different. The lesson content is something the students have to learn, but often don't want to. The act of engaging them in real learning requires that the teacher create a personal bond both with the group and with the individuals in the group. For each class and for the length of the course there is a full and rich common life between teacher and students.

The list of opportunities for common life in the workaday world is endless. We merely have to find them and recognize them as true outpouring of grace through which we are co-creators with God in the social reality of the world we inhabit together.

It is not enough simply to live together in the world, moving along whichever way the currents take us. We must swim beneath the surface of life to discover the richness of it all. Augustine was aware that his discovery of God at the deepest levels of his own soul was simply a microcosm of God's action in all of humanity. Each one of us is such a microcosm. Through prayer and attention to God's grace within us, we then extend in small, short and simple ways "in the rough and on the run," the common life that is already there.

If significant numbers of people committed themselves to living this way, perhaps the antidote to our collective narcissism would emerge. If we begin to flesh out our life together in such small ways as I have suggested, we find that we are beginning to act out the servant ministry of Jesus. God becomes more real to us and others become more important to us. We begin to perceive in ourselves, in our relationships and in every transaction with others the truth about Jesus that Augustine articulated so well and we can begin to apply it to our life together.

He is both great in the nature of God
and small in the form of a servant,
but in such way that his greatness
is not diminished by his smallness,
nor his smallness overwhelmed by his greatness.[21]

our common life

Five

Growing our Community to Include the World

My wife and I were standing in line to return some poorly-made items at a large chain store. At the service counter, a young woman was trying to wait on about half a dozen impatient and angry customers, attempting to answer telephone calls at the same time. She was obviously under great stress. Absorbing my wife's innate patience, I refrained from joining in the angry chorus of customer comments. When our turn came we thanked her for doing a difficult job. She was obviously shocked that we had said something nice to her. She blurted out::

"I'm only 20 years old and I'm about to have an aneurism because of the pressure around here. The company doesn't care about us employees. They won't hire enough people to work here because they want bigger profits."

Aside from the question of whether stress causes aneurisms, it seems she was right: the corporation really didn't care about its employees-or the customers either for that matter. I am beginning to believe that most management is interested only in the bottom line return on investment for their stockholders. They need employees, but they pay them as little as possible and have them do as much work as they can get out of them. I took the young woman seriously and decided to test out my hypothesis

Having noticed that there seem to be ever fewer employees in most large stores and supermarkets, I decided to do a little survey to find out whether others felt the same way about their jobs and their bosses. So I started to ask around. Sure enough, quite a few sales people and clerks told me the same thing. There are indeed fewer people working than there were a year ago, and no, the pay is not really any better. It's the old problem of "do more with fewer people." I am finding that the bottom line truly rules the retail world.

People who work for public agencies tell the same story. Because I am a retired federal employee and still work for my old health care agency once in awhile, I know first-hand that each provider has increasing case loads-with ever fewer providers available. Sometimes a real person at the other of an interminable telephone tree, someone who really wants to help, will apologetically admit that he or she is caught in the same bind.

My survey, which I continue to take at every opportunity, has resulted in a greater understanding of the burdens placed upon ordinary working people, most of whom are trying to do genuine customer service under adverse conditions. These people are part of my "community" in the widest possible sense. They are in that community because I choose to put them there. I choose to know them as people and I also choose to know something specific about them-in this case, their working conditions. I would have contact with these people anyway, but without the choice to include them in my loose community, they would remain just random people who happen to cross my path ever so briefly.

Augustinian spirituality, with its emphasis on love as the primary motivating force, gives a pre-eminent role to the human will and its choices. At the most basic level, we can choose even whether or not to know something. We can choose whether to know people only as useful objects-the means by which we achieve our own goals-or to know them as fellow children of God, equal in dignity to us and as companions for a moment along the way to God.

While standing in the customer service line, my wife made a choice not to become angry. For her this kind of choice is a habit. It's not a habit for me but I chose to follow her direction. That choice led to the kind words to the young woman behind the counter. Her response and her revelation of the pressures to which she was subjected allowed us to learn something about her and also something about other working people in similar situations. She became part of our larger community-every time we went into the store after that time, we would look for her and try to say hello-and she even became a "teacher," providing insights into the way this particular part of the world operates.

While we were having some remodelling work done on our home, we made it a point to listen to what members of the various trades had to say about their jobs, we watched how they worked and we learned something of them as people. Not only did they become part of our community, but we came to know something about their work beyond just what they did in our home. We now know much more about the trades, how they function and the pressures they face. What we know depends to a great extent on what we choose to know.

Learning On The Streets

Years ago, when I was working for the VA in Los Angeles, my job took me out on the road a lot and I spent a good deal of time in some poverty-stricken and rough areas of the city. As one sent out to solve specific VA-related problems, most often involving finances, I was forced-but also chose-to learn in great detail what really goes on in that great city. One can drive past these same areas on the freeways and never have a clue about what life is really like in those areas unless one chooses to take the off-ramp, drive into the area, park the car, get out and talk to people.

In our increasingly privatized, customized, cocooned lifestyle, we have fewer opportunities to truly know people different from ourselves and the conditions under which they live. We can even travel to foreign countries and see the sights, but unless we choose to really know the people there, we can come back with little more than some great pictures. Community in any Augustinian sense requires compassionate knowledge of people. This kind of knowledge requires choice.

If this sounds like a "theory of knowledge," it is-and it is one that is desperately needed in age when empirical verification, statistical analysis and vast amounts of computerized data are used to determine how work, what we do, how we think and even how we see ourselves. The knowledge of people is more basic than the knowledge of facts. If we see people only as facts and expect them to behave in ways derived from computerized data driven models, we are in serious trouble.

Traditionally, western civilization has understood knowledge to be an intellectual apprehension of reality. This is more abstract and distant than was the biblical understanding of knowledge. For the Hebrews, the biblical people of Israel, knowledge was a matter of the heart, the head, experience, intellect, will: all of the above. The New Testament, which was written in Greek for non-Jewish readers, incorporated some elements of Greek intellectual knowledge, combining it with the more dynamic Hebrew understanding of knowledge, but never losing the wider biblical perspective. We need to return to our biblical roots regain some of that vibrant outlook.

Augustine, though he was influenced by Greek philosophy, was fundamentally a Christian theologian. Scripture was the primary source for what he said and wrote. Using the Bible as a base, he was breathtakingly bold in his understanding of the dynamic interaction between intellect and will, between knowing and choosing. He believed that it is "the will or love which unites the knowing subject and the object known." He was convinced that there was no knowing without loving and no loving without knowing. Both knowing and loving belong equally and essentially in the mind. But he went even further than this. He saw in the intimate exchange between knowing and loving a faint echo or image of the way the Father and the Son are joined by the bond of love which is the Holy Spirit.[22]

As we progress in the intimate knowledge of God and of ourselves, we discover that God becomes the deepest center of our seeking, loving and knowing. But God has first loved the world and all humanity. For this reason, the sweep of our knowledge and loving expands to include as much of God's creation as we can. This is a truly radical extension of Augustine's foundational premise that the heart is restless until it rests in God. The fullest wisdom is to know (and thereby love) God, creation, our fellow humans and ourselves within this grand and all-encompassing embrace.

In the previous chapter, I suggested small steps: creating transitory moments of companionship at checkout lines and expanding these to longer-term relationships whenever possible. I now suggest that we can take a fresh look and operate differently within what seem to be purely functional and utilitarian relationships. We can choose to know-and hence to love-some particular aspect of a person who performs a utilitarian function for us, someone we would never otherwise get to know or care about. In situations where business transactions are increasingly constrained by computer-like speed and efficiency, taking the time and making the effort to engage another person as fully human and worthy of our love are decisive steps in another, a thoroughly Christian direction-one which is at odds with the manic speed of our culture

There is yet another step. We are immersed in reports, statistics, demographic trends and the use of rigorous scientific methodology. We do get from this flood of data some crucial information that we need to interpret and to take seriously. A large and complex society cannot operate without a continual and accurate data flow. The problem is that statistics are "out there". There is no face, no name, no person with whom to identify. We can "know" lots about the world in which we live by paying attention to charts and graphs, but we cannot really know it this way with any real wisdom. Choosing to know and to love others precisely in that place where efficiency rules and where the bottom line is lord is one small step along the way to recognizing that there really is another Lord who calls us all into a common life together.

My survey of busy and harried employees with too much to do gave me a much greater understanding of reports and statistics describing the number of hours Americans now work, the impact of outsourcing jobs, wage stagnation, poverty, homelessness and the like. I now know what the data means because the data describes people of flesh and blood, people with whom I share at least a shred of common life.

Choosing to know in this way enables me to know the wider worlds of American and global society more profoundly. Because knowledge and love are reciprocal, I am now able to love more widely than would be otherwise possible. This provides an expanded vision of what our life together is really all about.

If knowledge and choice are to be motivated by love, some action is usually required. An example comes to mind. During the years I worked for the Los Angeles VA, my job required me to find food and shelter for homeless veterans. There was a wide array of social services in the city, but I had to put something together for each individual through phone calls or personal contact. Many agencies had no telephone access after 5PM. Los Angeles County Social Services had an after hours number for people to use in emergencies, but I found that giving clients this number amounted to nothing more than a bureaucratic shuffle that yielded no real results. Subjecting people to this only increased their bitterness, kept them on the streets one more day and made their lives more difficult.

I found there were ways around this if you knew other telephone numbers, had personal contacts, and, in some instances if you could deliver the client personally. The problem was this all took place after normal working hours and there was no additional pay for working late. That's when I rediscovered what is for me the most uncomfortable passage in all of Scripture, one that I often wished had never been included: the Parable of the Good Samaritan. (Lk 10: 25-37)

The story is crystal clear. The priest and the Levite who pass by the injured man on the road had every good reason for doing so. The Samaritan had every reason for not acting mercifully, but he did so at considerable personal cost to himself. Jesus tells us that the Samaritan sets the standard for how we are to operate. Knowing the story quite well, I was unable to avoid the images in my imagination which sprang from my deep memory every time an after-hours client arrived at my desk. I could visualize in a fraction of a second the priest and the Levite passing by and the Samaritan stopping. I was than faced with a choice: which would I be? Would I give out the after hours number and pass on by this veteran or would I, like the Samaritan, actually do something?

Nothing in my job required me to stay a minute after closing and there were good reasons not to, but the Christian life demands more of us than our job requirements. So each time I was confronted with a choice: I could be the Samaritan or I could pass on by. Sometimes I was the priest or the Levite and sometimes I was the Samaritan. Whenever I chose to give out the phone number, telling the veteran that was all I could do, I felt most uncomfortable. As the years went by, the passage began to wear me down and I stayed to help more often.

The story of the Good Samaritan still haunts me in all kinds of situations. This is good because it forces me to make decisions and often to act in a more compassionate way than I otherwise would.

Not all of us wander the streets of LA or have a job at the VA. Sometimes your choice means making the choice to join with others in an existing helping community. Here's an example involving the judgement scene in Matthew's Gospel (Mt. 25:31-46), another troublesome passage.

I was once associated with a small Episcopal parish in Los Angeles which took its turn in rotation with six other churches in the area to make sure that homeless people in the area would have at least one good meal each day. Once a week, the cooking crew would assemble early in the morning and prepare a good meal, serving sometimes more than a hundred people. Some members of the cooking crew were in their 70s and 80s. I once asked them why they did it. One outspoken old gentleman asked if I had ever read the Bible. I replied that I had. He then asked if I was familiar with Matthew 25. I replied that I was. "What," he asked "did Jesus say to do for the hungry?" "Feed them," I said. To which he replied: "Then don't ask any more foolish questions."

I got the point. These people translated their faith into action on a regular basis. They had a disciplined spiritual life that included as a necessary component being on the weekly cooking crew to feed the homeless. They lived out their Bible.

Augustine was very clear. Common life means a complete sharing of all worldly possessions. In the first chapter of his Rule, he writes: "Call nothing your own, but let everything be yours in common. Food and clothing shall be distributed to each of you...not equally to all, for all do not enjoy equal health, but rather according to each one's need. For so you read in the Acts of the Apostles that they had all things in common and distribution was made to each one according to each one's need (4:32, 35)." He also writes: "It is better for us to want a little than to have too much."[23]

Augustine wrote the Rule for a specific religious community and not for the wider world, but common sharing of goods remained for him a fundamental principle of common life. When we apply this principle to the life together of the entire world community, the implications are staggering. Relentless poverty on a global scale, the growing divide between the very wealthy and all others, the dislocation of peoples, wars fought for resources, the plundering of the environment: imagine the world if a significant number of people really believed that, for the sake of the common good, "it is better for us to want a little than to have too much."

Augustine believed that the breakdown of the Roman Empire was due to its failure to live up to its own ideals. He speculated that it did not have the capacity to embody these ideals. Something more was needed, so he proposed a new premise as the foundation of society. He believed that society could not endure if it was based on simply abstract principles of justice. There must be a "common agreement on the things one loves."[24]

In an Augustinian frame of reference, we do not begin with abstract ideals of social justice and then proceed to economic and political action. We start with the knowledge and love of God and of our neighbors within the ambit of our own lives and extrapolate from there to the national and global arenas.

For those who would follow an Augustinian approach to the spiritual life, the way is clear to see and yet difficult to live. If the basis of our society is in fact a common agreement on what we love, and if we are called above all else to love God and then our neighbour, then there is no doubt about what we are to do. Our economic and political decisions are concentric circles that arise from "within our inmost parts" with God leading us on even there as "our helper."

We then choose to know and love even those with whom we have a passing relationship, extending to each and every one whatever we can of our common life with God. From this growing community, we learn more about each other and about God. In this way, our capacity to love grows. We find that we are able to see more clearly and act more forcefully in the larger society.

If we do all this in a disciplined and consistent fashion, as did those people on the cooking crew at the little church in Los Angeles, we find it becomes a kind of rule of life. With growing awareness of God "within our deepest parts" and God present also in everyone we meet, we are more at home in the world and more able to bring about change where it is needed. This is a rule of life which brings about great enjoyment of

God, ourselves, of others and of the world in which we live. It is a rule whose precepts are few and simple.

"The Lord grant that you may observe all these precepts in a spirit of charity as lovers of spiritual beauty, and may spread abroad the sweet odor of Christ by a good life: not as slaves living under the law but as men and women living in freedom under grace."[25]

william p. mahedy

Six

Small Communities

We were in a room at the San Diego VA Post Traumatic Stress Clinic. It was our weekly Monday morning combat vet group and we had just escaped the chaotic freeway driving of the morning rush hour. Combat vets are more aggressive than most people when some "nutcase" driving at reckless speed, swings over from another lane, cutting in front with inches to spare, looking for next opening. Rage is one of the many residual effects of combat that veterans in PTSD groups must confront. Freeway driving in southern California is an easy rage trigger.

We were getting ready for group by unwinding from our freeway stress by sharing a few comments: "I was tempted to go pedal to the metal to get the s.o.b.," and, "If I'd had my weapon with me, I'd have taken him out," and "I flipped him off." One of the vets smiled and said, "Let's make a deal: every time we get cut off we'll pray for the driver." We were stunned.

After some discussion, we agreed that we would try it. After all, the group was all about overcoming the combat rage that hangs on for years. This would be a major step in that direction. We decided that we would report to the group each week about our successes and failures in praying for drivers who cut us off.

In our weekly reports, I found that I, a fellow combat vet, but a priest and the one who was supposed to be leading the group, was less able than many of the other vets to pray for those who cut me off. This was a source of some mirth among the vets.

We kept to our commitment for the duration of the group. As time went on, the reports of our success and failures in attempting to pray for reckless drivers, opened doors to other failings and flaws within us. We became increasingly able to reveal these to each other with honesty, humility and openness. Praying for one's enemies provides entry into some deep dimensions of the spiritual life. We found this to be a powerful practice that impacted us deeply.

Reflecting back on the years of running groups for veterans with combat related PTSD, I realize that these were among the most profound experiences of community I have ever had. In one group, a veteran told us that he had been trained to kill, had done a lot of killing in Vietnam and that he now needed a spiritual boot camp, a basic training course that would provide him with a disciplined approach to becoming a peaceful man. He wanted to learn again how to relate to others without anger, to live in the present without his combat past haunting him. He wanted to rediscover God in his life. Other members in the group agreed with him and decided we needed to devise a spiritual basic training course.

Over the next three months, we did just that. We created a

twelve-step program, using the tools of Alcoholics Anonymous and other recovery programs, adapting the principles to the specific application to combat vets.

The vets loved it. Requests for spiritual boot camp soared and we were soon running multiple groups, struggling to keep up with the demand.

The veterans then began to request advanced training in "spiritual recovery alumni groups" when they had finished the three month boot camp. We also began to do meditation groups with the help of another clinician who was knowledgeable in the subject. The chaplain who replaced me when I retired continued these groups and branched out even further into different dimensions of the spiritual life.

For most of us, marriage and family are the most intense communities. For me, these have been the most satisfying, spiritually fruitful and enjoyable. So much as has already been written on this intimately personal dimension of life that I will omit any discussion of it in these pages.

I have served as a priest in many different parish churches, both Roman Catholic and Episcopalian. My wife and I have belonged to the same parish for more than twenty-five years. I am convinced that the parish church, of whatever Christian denomination, is a powerful source of community. There is no question that the parish, the fellowship of believers gathered regularly together in prayer, worship, friendship and service to others, is the primary community of Christianity.

Without the local church, there really is no Christian common life to extend out into the world. Again, much has been written, some of it quite good, about church life, so I will not consider it any further in this book.

Real community necessarily entails "face to face" relationships, with people interacting at all levels. The Augustinian hallmark of community-one founded in real bonds of friendship-is fully possible only in this kind of environment. Community extended to people in supermarket checkout lines and on the other edges of daily activity proves the power of common life when intentionally pushed beyond its normal boundaries. We must now focus on the primary vehicle of community that is the small group.

Augustine, lover and father and later pastor and bishop, was well aware of both family and the local church. But the rule he wrote for monastic life, most of his theological writing and the spiritual life of the Augustinian Order are all concerned with life beyond both the family and the local church. In that same spirit, I will continue to focus on this wider sweep of Augustinian life.

The veterans groups I ran toward the end of my career were similar to those that I had conducted during the 1970s and early '80s. Even in those early days, where the focus was on readjusting to civilian life, finding jobs and meeting immediate needs, there was an obvious spiritual dimension. Religious and moral issues always surfaced and the members of the groups formed a common bond. As one veteran put it in those days: "This group is my church."

It is true that veterans groups are to some degree an obvious substitute for the camaraderie found among soldiers in the field facing enemy fire. In combat, one bonds with others for sheer survival and there is no other relationship quite like it. Everyone who has ever served knows this and veterans groups become a kind of substitute for the camaraderie of combat.

The primary focus of combat soldiers is survival while accomplishing the mission. Veterans groups, if left to themselves, quickly deteriorate into swapping war stories-some of them stretching the truth-or may concentrate only on psychological survival. In veterans groups as elsewhere, there must be an intentional focus on forming a common life that takes one beyond the self, creating an opening to God and leading one to the service of others.

We progressed in the spiritual boot camp toward the twelfth and final step; there we discussed the "Greek god, GOYA." Who is GOYA? In the polite form, it is an acronym for "Get Off Your Anatomy." This was our way of understanding the story of the Good Samaritan. It also encapsulates Augustine's emphasis on the primacy of love in all things.

After years of conducting groups for combat veterans, I became aware that what I was really doing was living with them-and guiding them to go deeper into-the common life that I had lived in the Augustinian Order. All this was done with a good number of veterans who didn't believe in God or were angry with God, many of whom were suspicious and alienated, and a great many with drug and alcohol problems. The remarkable thing is that it worked.

In the spiritual recovery alumni groups, I began to make the

97

focus even more specific on our need to live some kind of a common life with all we meet. This must include, I told them, those who protested the war, government leaders and politicians, ex-wives, alienated parents and children, those who work in the VA, and people we simply don't like. Where before we were addicted to violence, we must now be bearers of mercy, peace, kindness and forgiveness. They realized that the wounds of war are healed only when the combat soldier becomes an instrument of peace.

One group even adopted the term "common life" and decided to do something to form a common life with people who run the large and often overwhelming VA healthcare system. They realized that there is not really even a common language to use in explaining the emotional and spiritual scars of war to most health care providers or VA staff. They adopted as their mission "developing a common language and a common life" between veterans and VA personnel.

They formed an organization they called American Combat Veterans of War (ACVOW) with the purpose of helping veterans navigate through the VA medical and compensation systems. They wanted to act as advocates for the veteran to the agency and explain the system to the veteran. Their goal was to obtain the full range of services in a timely fashion for the individual veterans and to make it easier for the VA to deal with sometimes hostile clients. Their goal was not only to get the job done, but to reduce stress levels by demonstrating to everyone in the process that there were common interests and that all were part of a larger community.

This venture began more than five years ago. ACVOW now

has office space within the San Diego VA Medical Center; they have gained new members and they are effective at their task. They are respected by VA personnel and are often asked by VA employees for assistance. Now they have begun to act as counsellors for some of the younger veterans. They have done this with no further guidance from me and they now have a five-year track record of putting into practice "a common language and a common life." The veterans groups remain for me a powerful example of what our life together should be.

Another impressive example of community life comes from some years ago while I was a campus minister and young adult pastor in San Diego. I had become aware that young people faced a range of psychological and spiritual problems far greater than those I had encountered growing up. Individualism had become more rampant, economic prospects had diminished, family and other support systems had disappeared and the culture was becoming more difficult for young people to navigate. Though I was aware of these changes, the full impact had not yet struck me.

My awakening occurred during the closing session of a weekend retreat with about sixty young adults in attendance. A woman in her early twenties admitted that she had very little to live for and had contemplated suicide. Others nodded in recognition of her anguish and the floodgates opened, with people pouring out their own pain. Before the session ended, I left in order to prepare for the closing worship service of the weekend. Another retreat leader, also a man of middle years, remarked to me, "It used to take sixty years to build up this kind of trauma, but now they do it in twenty.

Not long afterwards, our young adult group did a Bible study on Galatians 6:2: "Bear one another's burdens and in this way you will fulfill the law of Christ." The questions for discussion were: "What are your own burdens?" and "What are the burdens of others?" The outpouring was intense: sexual abuse, drug addicted and alcoholic parents, mothers and fathers who really didn't care, the pointlessness of life, the meaningless of education, a future with little more than low paying jobs. I was deeply troubled to discover that these were the realities of life for my young friends.

As a result of these experiences, the young adult community decided that they would become "the Galatians church," taking as their focal point the single verse that had been the catalyst at the Bible study. Over the course of the next few months, they became more intentional about inviting friends to the group, to our worship services and to community events. We had several competent musicians in the group and they began to select songs and hymns that reflected what they were trying to do. The community life changed, the bonds with one another were strengthened, prayer and worship became more important to them, and newcomers were not only invited but welcomed and made to feel completely at home.

As with the veterans group, it all began with a desire for friendship that included all who came into the community. As with the veterans, there was a commitment to transcend themselves and their own problems and to serve others. There was a very powerful prayer life and an obvious openness to God. The worship services reflected these elements and were among the most memorable services I have ever attended. For me, as for many of those young adults-now no longer as young-that community remains a most powerful example of what our life together as Christians should really be.

My experiences of community with veterans and with young adults were rich and full. With both groups, I found real honesty, humility, lack of pretension, openness to others and to God. I can think of no finer expressions of the common life as envisioned by Augustine and as lived by Augustinians down through the ages. Yes, it really does work if you try it. They gave it a try and, with God's grace, it worked magnificently.

One of my young colleagues in campus ministry explained that many people now view the world through a "prism of distrust." She explained that we must establish "pockets of resistance" to the culture, "where people come together in small groups to simply be with others they trust, with friends. Trust is a discipline that must be practiced." She believes that we must recapture "slowly and in a new dimension, the foundation of friendship-and all friendships begin in trust."[26]

For the veterans, the same idea is stated in Step Eleven of the Spiritual Recovery Program.

"We committed ourselves to completing the final mission of a combat soldier: becoming bearers of peace, prayerfulness, happiness and rejoicing, resolving to go behind the 'enemy lines' of fear, mistrust, selfishness, greed, hatreds which surround us in our culture, confident that, as warriors of peace, we will overcome these barriers using the weapons of peace, mercy and kindness which we have been given."

If young adults and combat veterans can form communities of friendship and trust as pockets of resistance behind the enemy lines of fear and mistrust in our culture, then anyone else can do it as well. This may in fact be what the entire Church is called upon to do in our time.

As Augustine said: "What consoles us in this human society, so full of errors and hardships, except unfeigned faith and the mutual love of good and true friends?"[27]

william p. mahedy

Seven

Tying It All Together

A ugustine did not buy into the prevailing idea of his time
(Cicero's) that based society upon justice. He did not, of
course, deny that justice is fundamental in societies, but he
insisted that, despite our best efforts, we are unable to attain
or sustain these ideals in practice. We simply do the best we
can, but we always end up "a long way from the perfection of
justice...a kind of lesser justice."[28] Society never can arrive at
perfect justice; it is always flawed. There is no such thing, for
example, as a completely just war or a fully just distribution of
wealth.

As Christians, we are morally bound to do the best we can in
our public and private lives, for we are bound by the impera-
tive of love. But we always fall short. We can never lay claim
to absolute justice either for ourselves or for our society. For
this reason there really is no truly unique or specific Christian
form of social organization.[29]

Knowing that we can't achieve perfection requires us to reori-
ent ourselves in the fractious debates now polarizing American
society on so many issues, e.g., the social role of the Christian
religion, the war in Iraq, the distribution of wealth, the culture

wars.

Augustine believed that love and friendship are more central to the social contract than abstract ideas are. This point of view differs radically from prevailing notions-which seem to have led us astray. It's time to try something new-which is really very old. But we must recognize that even a new course will always be tentative, imperfect and partial. We can only attempt to do what we believe is authentic and in accord with our Gospel vocation.

But how to follow this old-made-new radical approach? First, we must abandon the notion that our point of view is always absolutely correct. No one has perfect knowledge. There is always room for another insight. In a polarized society we hold on to our own positions as absolute truth. We demean and even dehumanize those who disagree with us-and sometimes we do this in the name of religion. Debate spills over into personal relationships. Ideology-political, cultural and religious-rather than factual information determines how we think, what we do and how we treat others.

When we realize with Augustine that, even with our best efforts we always fall short of perfect justice, we can no longer withhold from those with differing opinions the courtesy and respect that is their due.

Second, we must take a fresh and more realistic look at the political, economic and religious jargon that is now so simplistically bandied about. By examining them from an Augustinian perspective, we are able to demythologize and deconstruct them.

This allows us to replace shallow platitudes with serious discourse. From this perspective we can renew our commitment to treat others, even those who disagree with us, as potential friends. We are then able to chart a different course. We are called to act on the impulse of love at all times, in our public, no less than in our private lives.

Can we as individuals make a difference? Yes.

Paradoxically, the more independently we are able to operate as Christians whose "weight is our love," the more we are drawn into community with others. The more we seek God intimately within ourselves, the more we are pulled outward to the love and service of others. This paradox lies at the heart of our Christian faith and it is the specific hallmark of Augustinian spirituality.

The place to begin, as I have suggested in previous chapters, is to focus intently on the search for God. Personal prayer, Bible study and spiritual reading are crucial activities. Here we must always beware of confusing the self with God in a sort of spiritual narcissism. God is totally transcendent to us is and yet so intimate as to be grasped in some way as abiding within us. This is the bedrock of traditional Christian spirituality and no one articulated it better than Augustine. If we start by seeking God and not ourselves, we move toward God. Otherwise we end up in contemplation only of ourselves. Augustine provides a pattern in his *Confessions*. Though introspective, he was focused on God, not on himself in his spiritual journey.

To the practice of individual prayer recommended in the early chapters, I suggest adding the constant and habitual practice of friendship and kindly companionship. These are simply two sides of the single coin of God's grace. By incorporating people we encounter into our prayer, we include them within our spiritual horizon, binding them closer to ourselves in community. In this way we embed more deeply attitudes and habits of friendship toward all. We have begun to personalize the Augustinian principle that the social contract is based not on any abstraction, but on personal relationships and ultimately friendship.

The next steps take us a little further along. We join together in small groups in churches, neighborhoods, in recovery programs or at work. We gather with friends to share our spiritual journey in sincerity and humility. There are countless "programs" and resources offered by religious and secular organizations to assist in this process; some of these are good and some not, but really all it takes to form a group is people with some idea of what they intend to do. Community comes alive in a different way in such groups.

Too often churches and denominational bodies are overly concerned with "churchy" issues, e.g., who should be ordained, how the liturgy should be conducted, who has authority over whom, etc. Much discussion takes place around these questions, siphoning off people's spiritual energy, diverting it into channels that are really peripheral to the central core of the Gospel. It seems that precious little time and effort is devoted to fostering the kind of spiritual companionship I described in earlier chapters. The missionary outreach of the Church, its role of servant ministry and its "sacramental" presence as a sign of the risen Christ to the world depends upon the depth and commitment of the people of God, their openness to God's grace, and their willingness to treat each other with respect and affection.

I suggest that people take the initiative and form such groups within their parish churches. Extend the boundaries to include participation with people and parishes across denominational lines. Experience of different Christian traditions makes real and personal our membership in the universal Church, the one Body of Christ.

Participating with members of other religious faiths-and of no religious faith-on matters of common interest such as the environment, justice and peace-and including these others with one's prayer-embodies personally our membership in the world community.

In all this, we must be aware of the restless heart. As Scripture tells us: "Here we do not have an enduring city, but we are looking for the city that is to come." (Hebrews 13:12)

This was Augustine's theme in *The City of God*, but its first and most personal expression is found in his cry to God in the *Confessions*: "You have made us for yourself, and our heart is restless until it rests in you." Augustinian spirituality from its inception is inherently restless.

If we are never at rest but we know our final destination is with God, we are free to ride the waves of life wherever they may take us. We will no longer be afraid of meeting new friends and companions along the way. We will be able to extend compassionate companionship all the way from the briefest encounters to more intimate and enduring church communities and small groups. This kind of holy restlessness-which is also most appropriate in marriage and family life-is able to take us into new depths and unexplored spaces in our relationships.

If we know that our political and economic systems are themselves only transitory, we will not be afraid to challenge them, to tinker with them and to act boldly for change. The laws of physics may be immutable (and even that may be open to question), but the laws that govern society and the arrangements of the markets are not. We relate to God as finite and changeable creatures. We, and all that is earthly, are in constant flux on a journey toward God that is both individual and communitarian. Far from being a source of fear, this should embolden us for action. Again, the paradox, the more solidly we are grounded in community with God through prayer and with others in our common life together, the more able we are able to take bold individual action.

Surprise is a constant of human life. Old animosities may be surrendered and friendships created in their place. One such experience comes to mind. A delegation of twenty-one Americans had been invited to the Soviet Union in 1988. A private foundation had requested American assistance in aiding the Soviet veterans of the war in Afghanistan. These veterans were having trouble adjusting upon their return home. I was among those who agreed to go. Several of us were Vietnam veterans and we knew that the Russians were our surrogate enemies in Vietnam as we were theirs in Afghanistan. We did not know what to expect, but we went.

On our arrival at the airport, we were greeted by college student translators and young Russian veterans, most of whom
had never met an American. On our first day there a former
Russian soldier, Nicolai, who had lost a leg in Afghanistan was
talking to an American, Jack, who had been wounded in
Vietnam. Nicolai pointed to his prosthetic leg and said that he
had been wounded by an American-made machine gun. Jack
pointed to his body and said that he had been wounded by
shrapnel from a Russian-made rocket. They embraced as
Nicolai said, "My brother." In that moment of reconciliation
deep bonds of friendship were formed. Two years later it was
a privilege to have Nicolai visit as a guest in our home. One of
our translators has also visited our home several times. We
consider her "our Russian daughter". Yes, life is full of surpris-
es. Old antagonisms can die and friendships arise in their
place.

If everything old has passed away and everything has become
new (2 Cor 5:16), then there is a continual refashioning of ourselves, other people, all human systems and the cosmos itself.
God calls to us from the future, from the vantage point of the
risen Christ who stands at the end of time, drawing us ever
onward into that new creation which will be a "face to face"
common life together with God.

our common life

Eight

Our Life Together, Let Us Rejoice in It.

Augustine ended his autobiography, the *Confessions*, in what some people have considered a strange way: he added three chapters seemingly irrelevant to his personal story. These deal with time and memory (chapter 11), the Book of Genesis (chapter 12) and the Trinity (chapter 13). Gary Wills believes that Augustine did this because he was beginning to reassess his own personal story in the light of a much larger drama of which he had been previously unaware.[30]

It is only fitting to end this book by acknowledging that our personal stories and our life together are only part of a vast and sweeping cosmic drama which we now see in greater detail and scope than did the bishop of Hippo and his contemporaries who lacked the scientific tools we have. Though the science was lacking in that era, Augustine understood the significance of both time and the universal importance of numbers in the working of the cosmos. He knew that the book of Genesis did not "teach us how the heavens go, but how to go to heaven." He knew that living things contained within themselves "seminal reasons" implanted by God which would later develop into things we find in the world. He was also aware of the importance of the entire Trinity, God, Father, Son and Holy Spirit in the creation, renewal and destiny of the cosmos. These were to become for him dominant themes and the subject of his major works.

In the spirit of Augustine, let us end with a reflection upon Scripture in light of what we now know about the universe and our place in it.

"The heavens are telling the glory of God; and the firmament proclaims his handiwork. Day to day pours forth speech, and night to night declares knowledge. There is no speech, nor are there words; their voice is not heard; yet their voice goes out through all the earth and their words to the end of the world." (Psalm 19:1-4)

In a vast universe consisting of perhaps billions of galaxies with billions of stars each, we know that the cosmos is finite with a beginning point. Biological evolution, which is the source of so much controversy today, is really only a blip in the larger process of cosmic evolution. We have known for a hundred years that time and space are a single continuum and we know that everything in the universe is related to everything else. We have also learned that stars and planets operate differently than do the micro-particles which constitute everything in the universe.

We have learned that by conceding to the universe the autonomy and the randomness required by biological evolution-and even more by cosmology and particle physics-we discover dependencies within autonomy and patterns within randomness. We now recognize that though vast, the universe is not

112

only finite, it is also knowable, measurable, and it has a point of origin which is calculable. As to our role within the cosmos, we are able to understand it, to know something real about it.

What is truly remarkable is not that we have evolved from within it, but we are able to grasp it with our tiny intellect. Even if what we know is but a small speck of what could be known, it is still true that we can comprehend it with our minds. Augustine was fascinated with numbers and rightly so, for it turns out that we can predict what we will later empirically discover through what some have called "elegant equations." (Brian Green) This ability of puny minds to comprehend the cosmos and to operate freely within it is simply a working out of what we have learned from Scripture

"When I look at your heavens, the work of your fingers, the moon and the stars that you have established; what are human beings that you are mindful of them, mortals that you care for them?
Yet you have made them a little lower than God, and crowned them with glory and honor." (Psalm 8: 3-5)

Far from being diminished by the findings of science, we see more clearly who we really are in the hands of God. A wonderful summation of our place in the cosmos is found in the Book of Common Prayer and is used in Sunday worship by the Episcopal Church.

"At your command all things came to be: the vast expanse of interstellar space, galaxies, suns, the planets in their courses, and this fragile earth, our island home. By your will they were created and have their being. From the primal elements you brought forth the human race, and blessed us with memory, reason, and skill...."[31]

Far from being fearful of the findings of contemporary science, we should revel in them and allow ourselves to be delighted by the discoveries we make about the work of God. This was the spirit of Augustine and his intellectual heirs down to and including the present day.[32]

Our common life together with each other and with all humanity is connected to this vast expanse and it is most intimately connected with God who is transcendent to the entire cosmos. When we grasp the God of power and mystery, the *apophatic* aspect of God, we can then delight in the *kataphatic* "downsizing" of God. Like Augustine, we never cease to be amazed at the Eternal Word of God who: "Unspeakably wise, he is wisely speechless." The Augustinian spiritual life is one of unending wonder addressed to God: "For you were more inward to me than the most inward part of me and higher than my highest reach."

Finally, our common life together is a way to share, as adopted children, in that common life within the Trinity. It is this God, who has made all things new through Christ and the working of the Spirit, who calls to us from the future, from the new creation that has begun in the risen Christ. This is our hope. This is the life we live together. Let us rejoice in it.[32]

"The grace of the Lord Jesus Christ, the love of God, and the communion of the Holy Spirit be with all of you." (2 Cor: 14)

william p. mahedy

Bibliography and Endnotes

Primary Sources: St. Augustine

S, Aurelii Augustini *Opera Omnia: Patrologiae Latinae Elenchus*: www. augustinus.it. (The Complete Works of St. Augustine: Latin version. Order of St. Augustine Website, also some English translations at this website)

Secondary Sources

Anonymous Author. *The Cloud of Unknowing*. Edited and new introduction by William Johnston. Image/Doubleday. Garden City and New York, 1973

Burt, Donald X. O.S.A. *Day By Day With Saint Augustine*. Liturgical Press, Collegeville, 2006

Burt, Donald X. O.S.A. *Friendship and Society: An Introduction to Augustine's Practical Philosophy*. William B. Eerdmans Publishing Co., Grand Rapids, 1999.

Dodaro, Robert, O.S.A. "Sacramentum Caritatis Foundation of Augustine's Spirituality" in Orcasitas, Miguel Angel, O.S.A. *Rule and Constitutions of the Order of St. Augustine.* Augustinian Press, Villanova, 1991

Ennis, Arthur J. O.S.A. "The Hermit Tradition: Its Origins and Influence in Augustinian History" *Augustinian Heritage,* vol. 39, no. 2 (ed. Rotelle) Augustinian Heritage, Villanova 1993

Fitzgerald, Allan D., O.S.A. *et al* (ed) *Augustine Through the Ages: An Encyclopedia.* William B. Eerdmans Publishing Co., Grand Rapids, Cambridge, 1999

Gilson, Etienne, *The Christian Philosophy of St. Augustine,* Random House, New York, 1960

Haught, John F. *God After Darwin: A Theology of Evolution.* Westview Press, Boulder/London, 2000

John of the Cross, *The Ascent of Mount Carmel* in *The Collected Works of St. John of the Cross* Ed. Kieran Kavanaugh and Otilio Rodriguez, Washington, DC, Institute of Carmelite Studies 1979.

Mahedy, William and Bernardi, Janet. *A Generation Alone.* Intervarsity Press. Downers Grove, 1994.

McGinn, Bernard. *The Foundations of Christian Mysticism: Origins to the Fifth Century.* Crossroad, New York, 1995

McKibben, Bill. "The Christian Paradox: How a faithful

nation gets Jesus wrong." *Harpers Magazine.*
August 2005

Mohler, James A. S.J., *A Speechless Child is the Word of God,*
New City Press. New Rochelle, New York,

Orcasitas, Miguel Angel, O.S.A. *Rule and Constitutions of the
Order of St. Augustine.* Augustinian Press, Villanova, 1991

Peacocke, Arthur. *Theology for a Scientific Age.* SCM Press Ltd.
London, 1993

Pelikan, Jaraslov. *The Emergence of the Catholic Tradition (100-
600).* University of Chicago Press, Chicago, London, 1971

Peters, Ted. *God as Trinity: Relationality and Temporality in Divine
Life.* Westminster/John Knox. Louisville, 1993

Polkinghorne, John. *Science and Theology: An Introduction.*
SPCK/Fortress, London/Minneapolis, 1998

Rano, Balbino, O.S.A., ed. John E. Rotelle, O.S.A. *Augustinian
Origins, Charism, and Spirituality.* Augustinian Press, Villanova,
1994

Rotelle, John E. O.S.A et al (ed) *The Tagastan A Review of
Augustinian Spirituality and Tradition* vol. 31, no. 1 Augustinian
Friars of St. Thomas of Villanova, 1985

Rotelle, John E. O.S.A. ed. *Augustinian Spirituality and the
Charism of the Augustinians.* Augustinian Press, Villanova, 1995

Rotelle, John E. (ed) *Augustine Day by Day*, Catholic Book Publishing Co., New York, 1986

The Episcopal Church *The Book of Common Prayer.* Seabury Press, 1979

van Bavel, T. J., O.S.A. *The Basic Inspiration of Religious Life*, Augustinian Press, Villanova, 1996

Verheijen, Luc, O.S.A. *Saint Augustine: Monk Priest Bishop.* Augustinian Historical Institute, Villanova, 1978 (trans. Sr. Agatha Mary)

Wills, Garry. *Saint Augustine.* Lipper/Viking, New York, 1999

Wright, Nicholas Thomas. Various writings on Jesus, Paul and Other Articles. Guidance in the New Testament by a leading scholar. www.ntwrightpage.com

Zumkeller, Adolar, O.S.A. (trans.O'Connell) (ed. Rotelle) *Augustine's Rule.* Augustinian Press, Villanova, 1987

Endnotes

Citations from the writings of Augustine are from different sources: from authors listed in the bibliography, from other books, cards and papers, from online sources, many are from the English translations at the Augustinian website. I re-translated some and others I translated directly from the Latin. I have checked the passages quoted with the Latin edition of the *Opera Omnia*. (The Complete Works of St. Augustine: Latin version. Order of St. Augustine Website)

[1](Sermon 190:4)

[2](Sermon 204A)

[3](Sermon 187, 1)

[4](Sermon 117.3.5)

[5](*Confessions* 13.9.1)

[6](*Confessions* 7.10.16)

[7](*Explanation of the Psalms*: 41:7-10)

[8](*Confessions*, 3, 6.11)

[9](*Confessions* 10, 27)

[10](Soliloquies: 2.1.1).

[11]John of the Cross.) *The Ascent of Mount Carmel*. 16th Century)

[12](*The Cloud of Unknowing*. Anonymous Author, 14th Century)

[13](*On the Trinity*,7.6.12)

[14](*Confessions* 1.1)

[15] (*City of God* 11.25)

[16] (*Confessions* 10. 20, 29)

[17] (*Letter 130, 13*-cited in Burt, 1999, p67)

[18] (Dodaro in Rotelle, 1995 p46)

[19] (Comment. John to Parthians 1.9; 8.1.0 cit in Burt, 1999 p67)

[20] (Rule, Ch 1, citing Acts 4:32-35)

[21] (Sermon 187, 1)

[22] (*Trin.* 9.4.4; 14.6.8; 9.22; cited in *Augustine*, Fitzgerald *et. al.* 1999, pp845-851)

[23] (*Rule 3.5*)

[24] (*City of God* 19.24, *see also* Wills 1999, p.117 and Fitzgerald et.al. p.198.)

[25] (*Rule 8.48*)

[26] (Mahedy, Bernardi, p.97)

[27] (*City of God* 19.8 in Fitzgerald, 1999, p 373)

[28] (*Of the Spirit and the Letter.* 36:64-65)

[29] (*City of God*, 1.9.1, 4.4, 15,4,18.52.1, 19.24, 22.24.2; *see also* Fitz et al. 200-201, Wills, 117)

[30] (Wills, 91-96)

[31] (*Book of Common Prayer*, p370)

[32] (Suggested readings: Polkinghorne, Peacocke, Haught, Peters, Wright, etc.)

[33] (*On the Trinity*, 14. 18-19, also Fitzgerald, 1999, p.850)

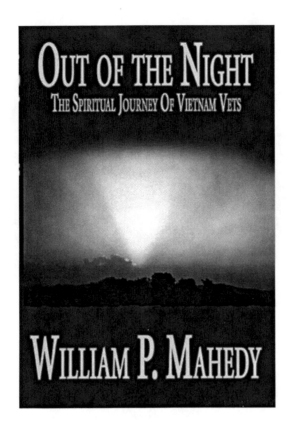

The classic guide to spiritual recovery for combat veterans, available from amazon.com or your local bookstore.

Fiction from Greyhound Books

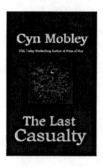

THE LAST CASUALTY
Cyn Mobley

A dying spy. A deathbed confession. How far will a Navy priest go to keep his vows? Bestselling author Cyn Mobley takes the reader inside the complex world of ancient vows and duty.

PROPHETS REBORN
Gary Gablehouse

Stolen holy relics and a plot to destroy the religious faith of billions. Anthropologist Gabe Turpin dives deep into the esoteric world of martial arts and Eastern mysticism to prevent the ultimate jihad.

685922

Made in the USA